SO-CJP-835

New Directions for
Student Services

John H. Schuh
EDITOR-IN-CHIEF

Elizabeth J. Whitt
ASSOCIATE EDITOR

Using Entertainment Media in Student Affairs Teaching and Practice

Deanna S. Forney
Tony W. Cawthon
EDITORS

Number 108 • Winter 2004
Jossey-Bass
San Francisco

USING ENTERTAINMENT MEDIA IN STUDENT AFFAIRS TEACHING AND PRACTICE
Deanna S. Forney, Tony W. Cawthon (eds.)
New Directions for Student Services, no. 108
John H. Schuh, Editor-in-Chief
Elizabeth J. Whitt, Associate Editor

NEW DIRECTIONS FOR STUDENT SERVICES (ISSN 0164-7970, e-ISSN 1536-0695) is part of The Jossey-Bass Higher and Adult Education Series and is published quarterly by Wiley Subscription Services, Inc., A Wiley Company, at Jossey-Bass, 989 Market Street, San Francisco, California 94103-1741. Periodicals Postage Paid at San Francisco, California, and at additional mailing offices. POSTMASTER: Send address changes to New Directions for Student Services, Jossey-Bass, 989 Market Street, San Francisco, California 94103-1741.

New Directions for Student Services is indexed in College Student Personnel Abstracts and Contents Pages in Education.

Microfilm copies of issues and articles are available in 16mm and 35mm, as well as microfiche in 105mm, through University Microfilms Inc., 300 North Zeeb Road, Ann Arbor, Michigan 48106-1346.

SUBSCRIPTIONS cost $75 for individuals and $170 for institutions, agencies, and libraries. See ordering information page at end of book.

EDITORIAL CORRESPONDENCE should be sent to the Editor-in-Chief, John H. Schuh, N 243 Lagomarcino Hall, Iowa State University, Ames, Iowa 50011.

Jossey-Bass Web address: www.josseybass.com

CONTENTS

1

This chapter addresses considerations related to and potential contributions of entertainment media use in student affairs learning contexts.

Introduction to Entertainment Media Use

Deanna S. Forney

My first attempt at using the media to facilitate student learning dates back to the mid-1980s when I was asked by a dean's office staff member at the small liberal arts college where I worked to consider doing a workshop on student development theory for the resident assistants and hall directors, all undergraduates, during their fall training. She related her efforts to teach Arthur Chickering's theory (Chickering, 1969) to this group the year before and how she did not believe the connections happened—that is, the students did not "get" the theory—and thus the theory's value as a resource wasn't established. I agreed to undertake this task, in part because the previous year, my own first attempt to teach student development theory to undergraduates—students in a peer counseling class at my doctoral institution—had also bombed.

Believing that student development theory could be a valuable tool for undergraduate staff and student leaders in understanding and responding to their peers, I wanted to try again to devise an approach that would effectively convey both the content and value of this body of knowledge. It turned out that the film *Revenge of the Nerds* (1984) held the key. I happened to see this movie on cable television at the time when I was planning the workshop, and I had an "aha" experience. I used the film to provide a common frame of reference that the student staff and I could use to make theory concrete and to provide examples that would be comprehensible to everyone. The students watched the film the night before our session, and we had fun using it to examine adjustment and identity issues, especially how these issues demonstrated connections to the theories of Maslow

1

(1954), Chickering (1969), and Schlossberg (1984). The approach worked effectively (Forney, 1986), and my interest in entertainment media as vehicles for promoting student learning began.

This sourcebook represents my most recent effort to reflect on and promote the use of entertainment media both in the classroom and in the more informal learning settings of student affairs, such as retreats and workshops. This introductory chapter will discuss the rationales for and other considerations related to entertainment media use.

Why Bother with Entertainment Media in Facilitating Learning?

For many college students, learning methods consist of reading assignments, lectures, papers, examinations, and group projects. Traditional means of learning certainly are valuable; however, reaching all students and enhancing their learning can necessitate going beyond the traditional, especially in the out-of-classroom environments that are typical in student affairs. In addition, entertainment media can provide learning opportunities that would be difficult or impossible to create through traditional means. For example, students can view a client's progress in counseling over several sessions in a two-hour film such as *Good Will Hunting* (1997) as opposed to actual observation that would take months in real life, if it was even possible. Or students can watch, in the film *American History X* (1998), the extreme example of the main character's development over time from a racist perspective to a white identity that rejects racism. Learning styles and other pedagogical considerations, student characteristics, and possible contributions of the media to learning all warrant attention in considering the value of using entertainment media.

Learning Style and Other Pedagogical Considerations. David Kolb (1984), in his theory of experiential learning, defines learning as "the process whereby knowledge is created through the transformation of experience" (p. 38). He describes learning as a four-stage cycle: concrete experience (CE), the feeling dimension; reflective observation (RO), the watching dimension; abstract conceptualization (AC), the thinking dimension; and active experimentation (AE), the doing dimension.

Learners need all four of these abilities to be effective in the learning process. The abilities of concrete experience (CE) and abstract conceptualization (AC) are considered polar opposites, as are the abilities of active experimentation (AE) and reflective observation (RO), and learners will prefer one ability over the other in each of these pairs. The CE-AC choice indicates a preference related to how one grasps or takes in information, and the AE-RO choice indicates a preference for how one processes information or makes it meaningful. Based on an individual's preference in each of these pairs, his or her learning style—that is, his or her typical way of responding to a learning situation—is identified.

Kolb (1984) labels these four learning styles as: *diverger* (CE and RO), imaginative, feeling-oriented, people-oriented, sensitive to meaning and values, skilled at viewing situations from multiple perspectives and generating alternatives and analyzing them; *assimilator* (RO and AC), preferring an idea focus over a people focus, skilled at inductive reasoning, and integrating ideas and creating theories; *converger* (AC and AE), preferring technical tasks over social or interpersonal contexts, skilled at deductive reasoning, applying ideas to practical situations, and making decisions; and *accommodator* (AE and CE), action-oriented, at ease with people, comfortable taking risks, skilled at carrying out plans and adapting to new situations.

Smith and Kolb (1986), Svinicki and Dixon (1987), and Pearson and Royse (2001) provide examples of learning activities that match the nature of each of the four learning style components. Following are some of the preferred learning activities that Smith and Kolb identify:

CE: new experiences; games; role plays; peer discussion and feedback; personalized counseling
RO: lectures; observation; exposure to different perspectives on an issue
AC: theory readings; study time alone; clear, well-organized presentations of ideas
AE: practice and feedback; small-group discussion; individualized, self-paced learning activities

Some additional examples from Svinicki and Dixon are the following:

CE: films
RO: journals
AC: analogies
AE: simulations

Pearson and Royse include

CE: storytelling
RO: brainstorming sessions
AC: writing critiques
AE: case studies

For a more detailed discussion of learning styles, see Kolb's work (Kolb, 1981, 1984) and the chapter on Kolb's theory in Evans, Forney, and Guido-DiBrito, 1998.

Media use has the potential to engage students in each of the four learning components. For example, watching a film or television clip or listening to music provides a concrete experience for students. Asking students to think about and process how the clip or piece of music demonstrates or connects to the course content under consideration engages them in reflective observation. Having students analyze the film clip and come up with their own related ideas (for example, what do they think is going on with the characters involved?) encourages abstract conceptualization. Finally, asking students how they would approach the situation or the characters presented in the clip encourages active experimentation. Coupling this type of approach with other learning activities such as reaction papers, journals, and group discussions (in person or electronically) further engages students in diverse learning activities.

Kolb (1984) emphasizes the importance of helping students develop all four learning abilities so that they can function in college and later in learning situations that impose different demands on the learners' skills. Flexibility and adaptability are important. Both support and challenge are needed. In other words, some activities that match an individual's learning style (the preferred two modes from CE-AC and AE-RO) help connect the student to the learning process, but some activities that encourage development of nonpreferred modes are also important. Most student groups within and outside the classroom are likely to include people with all four learning styles; therefore, including learning activities from all four modes provides challenges and supports in a class, program, or training session. In regard to graduate teaching, the potential for the population of master's candidates in student affairs to consist of many accommodators (Forney, 1994) implies that use of entertainment media can be especially effective with this group in making the abstract more concrete.

Brookfield and Preskill (1999) note the value of concrete images for visual learners and the general value of changing pace and format to accommodate different learning styles. Campoux (1999) indicates that some research suggests that individuals "learn abstract, new and novel concepts more easily when presented in both verbal and visual form" (p. 209).

Seyforth and Golde (2001) also cite cognitive implications of using entertainment media in instruction. They discuss the potential of film use to promote self-authorship (Baxter Magolda, 2001). Films can help students "find a personal connection to course material" (p. 4), thereby situating learning in the students' own experiences; connect themes to their own lives, thereby validating students as knowers; and facilitate their making meaning together with their teachers.

Student Characteristics. Seyforth and Golde (2001) state, "Contemporary college students are immersed in a popular culture that is largely defined by television and movies" (p. 3). This millennial generation is described by Howe and Strauss (2000) as "the most catered-to kids in the history of pop culture" (p. 250) in terms of the media's accommodation of their interests from childhood through adolescence. Especially for this generation, entertainment media can be powerful tools for teaching because of their ability to connect with students and engage them in the learning process, whether the learning occurs in a classroom or on a residence hall floor.

Light (2001), presenting the findings of his research with students at Boston area colleges, states that in regard to academics, "the most common hope students express is that each class, by its end, will help them to become a slightly different person in some way. This hope transcends the subject matter of a class, or a student's background, or even whether the student is a wise old senior or an incoming freshman" (p. 47). Newton (2000), discussing his research with Kansas State University students, advocates in-class and out-of-class opportunities that promote "student personal awareness and exploration" (p. 13) and exploration of "the meaning and purpose of their life activity" (p. 14). Use of the entertainment media has the potential to have an impact on students' affective and reflective capacities as well as address content knowledge attainment in and out of the classroom.

While the goal of using entertainment media is to teach rather than simply entertain, these media also have the potential to respond to Lancaster and Stillman's perception that as a consequence of the playful attitudes and multitasking skills evident in the millennial generation, speed and fun are facilitative, as is experiential learning (Lancaster and Stillman, 2002).

How the Entertainment Media Can Contribute to Learning

Hinton (1994) observes, "for a substantial segment of society, media substitutes for personal experience" (p. 2), and Campoux (1999) maintains that films, for example, "are an economical substitute for other real world visits" (p. 213). These are a couple of examples of what others have to say about the role and value of entertainment media in our lives.

Film use in teaching and learning has received more attention in the literature than has the use of television, music, or popular books. Clearly, avenues for further development are open in regard to all four media forms, but work with the latter three vehicles especially has the potential to add to our understanding of their effective usage in student affairs. Examples provided in the following chapters of this sourcebook often represent pioneering efforts in using television, music, and popular books in teaching and training.

Use of Film. In this volume, only films that were initially produced for entertainment rather than educational purposes are included. Numerous authors in the social sciences extol the virtues of film use in instruction. Wedding and Boyd (1999) observe that film is an integral part of our culture, a mirror in which we see ourselves. Boyatzis (1994) maintains that "movies tell a story and offer a powerful aesthetic experience" (p. 100) and for these reasons alone can be an effective teaching tool.

Film use has several purposes in training and teaching. Perhaps their most basic use is to present information (Koch and Dollarhide, 2000). Films integrate the practical and the didactic (Nissim-Sabat, 1979), illustrating substantive issues (Fleming, Piedmont, and Hiam, 1990) and making course topics "immediate, relevant, and concrete" (Anderson, 1992, p. 155). Films can give a visual portrayal of the abstract, providing a feeling of reality and showing how concepts are applied (Campoux, 1999). They can serve as a vehicle for exploring students' reactions and experiences (Koch and Dollarhide, 2000) and add to the impact of cognitive insight (Hesley and Hesley, 1998).

Films can provide common images and a common framework to support discussion of difficult subjects; they also grab the audience's attention "viscerally and quickly" (Seyforth and Golde, 2001, p. 3), holding and directing the attention of the viewer (Campoux, 1999). Films often address the affective realm (Hesley and Hesley, 1998), engaging students' feelings in addition to their thinking capacities. Films can aid in gaining insight into self and relationships, which can lead to "altered thoughts, feelings, and behaviors" (Heston and Kottman, 1997, p. 99).

Films can energize a group (Koch and Dollarhide, 2000), encourage engagement in discussion (Anderson, 1992), and enhance rapport between the group and instructor (Koch and Dollarhide, 2000). They can improve students' skills in taking different or new perspectives (Anderson, 1992). Films can give a longitudinal perspective or build a "bridge to the world of action" (English and Steffy, 1997, p. 114).

While the preceding comments were made about films specifically, many of the statements could also be applied to the use of other entertainment media.

Use of Television Shows. Some television shows may be useful because they portray characters and themes to which students can relate. For example, Schlozman (2000) notes that the characters in *Buffy the Vampire Slayer* depict important adolescent themes such as "the ego strength necessary to negotiate the developmental maze of adolescence" (p. 50).

Access to television shows can be an issue. However, television series are increasingly being released in DVD format (for example, *Felicity, My So-Called Life, Friends*), affording easier access. The more limited access to television shows may be one reason that films are typically used more extensively.

Use of Music. White (1985) describes the value of music as a means of communication with counselees. He also maintains that popular music can be a coping mechanism for young people who are dealing with the challenge of establishing and maintaining their identity. White's ideas seem relevant in regard to the meanings that popular music has for many college students. Tapping into this resource represents a different way to aid students in connecting to content.

Use of Popular Books. For our purposes, popular books are those written for a mass or general audience rather than an academic audience. Gladding (1994) describes the value of literature as a "nonthreatening means of conveying information to people about human nature and values" (p. 191) and also laments its underutilization in classroom instruction. Gladding, in the context of teaching family counseling, identifies four reasons for incorporating fiction into teaching: increasing awareness of emotions, understanding course content more fully, creating the potential for new insights or "aha experiences" (p. 193), and promoting compassion. Any of these reasons could also apply in student affairs content areas.

Levine and Shapiro encourage higher education personnel to read *Harry Potter and the Sorcerer's Stone* (Rowling, 1997) because of the connections they see to several campus themes such as "diversity, first-year experience, learning communities, good practice in teaching and learning, and civic responsibility" (Levine and Shapiro, 2000, p. 9) and the insights offered. A logical next step would be using this book in learning contexts with students. For example, if *Harry Potter and the Sorcerer's Stone* was included on the reading list for a freshman orientation or first-year experience, questions such as "How is the experience of entering college like Harry and his friends entering Hogwarts school?" could be asked.

For graduate students in an Introduction to College Student Affairs course, the book could prompt discussion about parallels between the experiences of Harry and his friends and the college experience, including the students' own undergraduate experiences. Use of the book in such contexts could provide a common frame of reference for exploring student perspectives on college life. Numerous other works of fiction could also serve this purpose.

Nonfiction works can bring "outside world" reality into the educational setting. For example, the use of biographies can provide concrete evidence of how theoretical concepts work, as Boyatzis (1992) demonstrates in his use of Maya Angelou's work as a vehicle for checking students' understanding of child development theory. He cites literature's value as residing in its personal, subjective experiences.

Works that focus on adolescent and adult development can be used to facilitate understanding of developmental theories pertaining to college students. For example, using *The Autobiography of Malcolm X* (Malcolm X, 1964) can be effective in promoting students' understanding of racial identity development theory.

Younger (1990), in discussing the relevance of literary works to nursing, states, "Good books can be a gift of wisdom to our students—the experience of life without its costs" (p. 42). This vicarious experience can be valuable for our students in student affairs learning contexts.

Some Suggestions for Using Entertainment Media Effectively

Several authors have offered suggestions related to the use of entertainment media in teaching and learning. Recognizing that the media may be used for different purposes, techniques for effective use will vary, depending on instructional goals and characteristics of each group of learners. Making media use an active rather than passive experience for students is important, however, to avoid students' disengaging during an extended video clip, for example.

Laying the groundwork, preparing the group prior to media use, is advisable (Summerfield, 1993). Purposes and expectations need to be clear. For example, stimulus questions (Koch and Dollarhide, 2000) or observation guides (Dorris and Ducey, 1978) can be provided to students prior to viewing a film or listening to music. Such structured supports make sense when goals relate to having students identify certain points or examples, reflect on specific questions, or analyze in a specific fashion. An alternate approach is have students view a clip or listen to music and attach their own meaning (Anderson, 1992). Lacey (as cited in Summerfield, 1993) recommends the image-sound skim technique as a way to begin discussion if a film is seen in its entirety. This technique involves asking students, at the conclusion of the film, to identify the images or sounds that immediately come to mind. The facilitator can then begin the discussion with the aspects that had an impact on the audience.

Campoux (1999) describes the use of films both before and after presentation of content information. With the former, students are given a visual image that can be referenced in explaining concepts. With the latter, students have an opportunity to apply what they have learned. With sensitive material, allowing students to begin the discussion by expressing their feelings prior to engaging in more intellectual tasks can be useful (Summerfield, 1993).

Media use may also take the form of homework assignments (for example, viewing a film prior to a class or training session or doing a journal entry based on a film) or graded assignments (for example, viewing a film, then writing a paper [Boyatzis, 1994] or taking an exam [Tyler & Reynolds, 1998] based on it). Furthermore, students can be asked to identify or supply their own relevant examples from entertainment media (for example, select a popular book or film and analyze it in regard to course or workshop content).

As Campoux (1999) states, the use of multiple media is a viable option that can reinforce learning in different forms. Also, student choice as to media format (book, film, and so on) for a given assignment has the potential to challenge or support on an individual level.

Evaluation of media use is important and can be done in a variety of ways. While Campoux (1999) presents empirical evidence of the positive impact of using films, our understanding of the impact of media use in regard to our own students is most meaningful. Possible forms of evaluation include observation (for example, increased class participation on the part of class members who previously have contributed less; use of concepts from media examples in student papers and exams); discussion with students (for example, soliciting informal verbal feedback on the impact of media use); and written (for example, items on formal course or workshop evaluations; five-minute in-class essays at the end of a class period on the impact of specific media use). Summerfield (1993) also suggests the use of the same exercise before and after viewing a film, for example, as a way for both facilitators and students to try to gauge the impact of using the media. Free association represents one type of pre/post activity (for example, "What do you think when you hear the term *Native American?*").

Some cautions regarding entertainment media use are also important to mention. Pardeck (1994) advocates selectivity in the use of literature to aid adolescent coping. It is appropriate to extend this caution to all entertainment media use with college students. As Tyler and Reynolds (1998) report, overuse can "create a blur" (p. 17). In other words, a stimulus overload can occur for students.

In addition, entertainment media use needs to be purposeful. I have observed more than one graduate student presentation, for example, in which entertainment media use seems token (that is, "to say we did"). Sufficient grounding in and connection to the content often does not occur. Meaningful use, which includes carefully selected items that are presented and explored in depth, is recommended rather than media blitzes or marginally related, minimally analyzed material.

Demerath (1981) warns that films can be "pedagogical booby traps" (p. 69). As Campoux (1999) states, films are fiction, and films easily lend themselves to propaganda in terms of their point of view, which can be biased rather than objective (Anderson, 1992). Avoiding stereotypes (Tyler and Guth, 1999) can be a challenge. Also, the entertainment media can contain disturbing elements in regard to violence, language, and so on. Students need to be cautioned (Anderson, 1992) or perhaps even given the option not to participate in the experience.

Finally, ethical use of entertainment media is important. Honoring copyright restrictions is one example; Campoux (1999) provides a more detailed discussion of related considerations.

Sourcebook Content and Goals

This sourcebook focuses on using films, television shows, music, and popular books to facilitate student learning. The goal is to share creative and effective approaches to reaching students in content areas that are frequently the focus in student affairs undergraduate and graduate courses, programming, and staff training. This volume is intended to be a resource for both student affairs practitioners and student affairs faculty as well as faculty in other disciplines in which the content areas may be relevant. The chapters that follow discuss the use of entertainment media to facilitate understanding of general student development, multiculturalism, sexual orientation, gender issues, leadership, counseling skills, and career development. The sourcebook concludes with a discussion of media resources and final suggestions for employing them effectively.

References

American History X. [motion picture]. United States: New Line Cinema, 1998.

Anderson, D. D. "Using Feature Films as Tools for Analysis in a Psychology and Law Course." *Teaching of Psychology,* 1992, *19*(3), 155–158.

Baxter Magolda, M. B. *Making Their Own Way.* Sterling, VA: Stylus, 2001.

Boyatzis, C. J. "Let the Caged Bird Sing: Using Literature to Teach Developmental Psychology." *Teaching of Psychology,* 1992, *19*(4), 221–222.

Boyatzis, C. J. "Using Feature Films to Teach Social Development." *Teaching of Psychology,* 1994, *21*(2), 99–101.

Brookfield, S. D., and Preskill, S. *Discussion as a Way of Teaching.* San Francisco: Jossey-Bass, 1999.

Campoux, J. E. "Film as a Teaching Resource." *Journal of Management Inquiry,* 1999, *8*(2), 206–217.

Chickering, A. W. *Education and Identity.* San Francisco: Jossey-Bass, 1969.

Demerath, N. J., III. "Through a Double-Crossed Eye: Sociology and the Movies." *Teaching Sociology,* 1981, *9*(1), 69–82.

Dorris, W., and Ducey, R. "Social Psychology and Sex Roles in Films." *Teaching of Psychology,* 1978, *5*(3), 168–169.

English, F. W., and Steffy, B. E. "Using Film to Teach Leadership in Educational Administration." *Educational Administration Quarterly,* 1997, *33*(1), 107–115.

Evans, N. J., Forney, D. S., and Guido-DiBrito, F. *Student Development in College: Theory, Research, and Practice.* San Francisco: Jossey-Bass, 1998.

Fleming, M. Z., Piedmont, R. L., and Hiam, C. M. "Images of Madness: Feature Films in Teaching Psychology." *Teaching of Psychology,* 1990, *17*(3), 185–187.

Forney, D. S. "Helping Undergraduate Residence Staff Use Theory to Support Practice." *Journal of College Student Personnel,* 1986, *27*(5), 468–469.

Forney, D. S. "A Profile of Student Affairs Master's Students: Characteristics, Attitudes, and Learning Styles." *Journal of College Student Development,* 1994, *35*(5), 337–345.

Gladding, S. T. "Teaching Family Counseling Through the Use of Fiction." *Counselor Education and Supervision,* 1994, *33*(3), 191–200.

Good Will Hunting [motion picture]. United States: Miramax Films, 1997.

Hesley, J. W., and Hesley, J. G. *Rent Two Films and Let's Talk in the Morning: Using Popular Movies in Psychotherapy.* New York: Wiley, 1998.

Heston, M. L., and Kottman, T. "Movies as Metaphors: A Counseling Intervention." *Journal of Humanistic Education and Development,* 1997, *36*(3), 92–99.

Hinton, D. B. *Celluloid Ivy: Higher Education and the Movies 1960–1990.* Metuchen, N.J.: Scarecrow Press, 1994.

Howe, N., and Strauss, W. *Millennials Rising: The Next Great Generation.* New York: Vintage Books, 2000.

Koch, G., and Dollarhide, C. T. "Using a Popular Film in Counselor Education: *Good Will Hunting* as a Teaching Tool." *Counselor Education and Supervision,* 2000, *39*(3), 203–210.

Kolb, D. A. "Learning Styles and Disciplinary Differences." In A. W. Chickering (ed.), *The Modern American College: Responding to the New Realities of Diverse Students and a Changing Society.* San Francisco: Jossey-Bass, 1981.

Kolb, D. A. *Experiential Learning: Experience as the Source of Learning and Development.* Englewood Cliffs, N.J.: Prentice Hall, 1984.

Lancaster, L. C., and Stillman, D. *When Generations Collide.* New York: Harper Business, 2002.

Levine, J. H, and Shapiro, N. S. "Hogwarts: The Learning Community." *About Campus,* 2000, *5*(4), 8–13.

Light, R. J. *Making the Most of College: Students Speak Their Minds.* Cambridge, MA: Harvard University Press, 2001.

Malcolm X. *The Autobiography of Malcolm X.* New York: Basic Books, 1964.

Maslow, A. H. *Motivation and Personality.* New York: HarperCollins, 1954.

Newton, F. B. "The New Student." *About Campus,* 2000, 5(5), 8–15.

Nissim-Sabat, D. "The Teaching of Abnormal Psychology Through the Cinema." *Teaching of Psychology,* 1979, 6(2), 121–123.

Pardeck, J. T. "Using Literature to Help Adolescents Cope with Problems." *Adolescence,* 1994, 29(114), 421–427.

Pearson, C., and Royse, D. "Teaching Students How to Learn." In Royse, D. (ed.), *Teaching Tips for College and University Instructors.* Boston: Allyn & Bacon, 2001.

Revenge of the Nerds [motion picture]. Hollywood, CA: Twentieth Century Fox, 1984.

Rowling, J. K. *Harry Potter and the Sorcerer's Stone.* New York: Scholastic, 1997.

Schlossberg, N. K. *Counseling Adults in Transition.* New York: Springer, 1984.

Schlozman, S. "Vampires and Those Who Slay Them: Using the Television Program *Buffy the Vampire Slayer* in Adolescent Therapy and Psychodynamic Education." *Academic Psychiatry,* 2000, 24(1), 49–54.

Seyforth, S. C., and Golde, C. M. "Beyond *The Paper Chase:* Using Movies to Help Students Get More Out of College." *About Campus,* 2001, 6(4), 2–9.

Smith, D. M., and Kolb, D. A. *User's Guide for the Learning Style Inventory.* Boston: McBer, 1986.

Summerfield, E. *Crossing Cultures Through Film.* Yarmouth, Maine: Intercultural Press, 1993.

Svinicki, M. D., and Dixon, N. M. "The Kolb Model Modified for Classroom Activities." *College Teaching,* 1987, 35(4), 141–146.

Tyler, J. M., and Guth, L. J. "Using Media to Create Experiential Learning in Multicultural and Diversity Issues." *Journal of Multicultural Counseling and Development,* 1999, 27(3), 153–169.

Tyler, J. M., and Reynolds, T. "Using Feature Films to Teach Group Counseling." *Journal for Specialists in Group Work,* 1998, 23(1), 7–21.

Wedding, D., and Boyd, M. A. *Movies and Mental Illness: Using Films to Understand Psychopathology.* Boston: McGraw-Hill College, 1999.

White, A. "Meaning and Effects of Listening to Popular Music: Implications for Counseling." *Journal of Counseling and Development,* 1985, 64(1), 65–69.

Younger, J. B. "Literary Works as a Mode of Knowing." *IMAGE: Journal of Nursing Scholarship,* 1990, 22(1), 39–43.

DEANNA S. FORNEY is professor of college student personnel in the Department of Educational and Interdisciplinary Studies at Western Illinois University in Macomb, Illinois.

2

This chapter sets a context for the use of student development theory in student affairs work, summarizes several prominent theories, and offers examples of how the entertainment media can be used to facilitate understanding of these theories by both graduate and undergraduate students.

Using Entertainment Media to Inform Student Affairs Teaching and Practice Related to Student Development Theory

Merrily S. Dunn, Deanna S. Forney

From the earliest articulation of student affairs' guiding principles, student affairs practitioners have clearly stated the necessity of educating the whole person ("The Student Personnel Point of View, 1937," 1983). The central idea of holistic education is that the conception and implementation of education must extend beyond teaching content in a classroom to other parts of student life.

To merit consideration as a legitimate profession, student affairs must have a theoretical foundation to undergird, support, and justify the structure, content, and practice of the work. Thus, student affairs practice needs to be grounded in relevant theory and validated through assessment. This necessity, coupled with the strong principle of holistic education, leads to the adoption of theories relevant to the psychosocial and cognitive structural development of traditional-age college students as a guiding theoretical construct for the profession.

Some of these theories were developed with traditional-age college students as their sample, while others were more broadly normed but found to be applicable to student populations. Arthur Chickering's initial theory of students' psychosocial development (Chickering, 1969) and the revision

Merrily Dunn wishes to thank George Thompson at the University of Georgia and Steve Kremer at The Ohio State University for their assistance.

13

and elaboration of this theory (Chickering and Reisser, 1993); Perry's theory of intellectual development (Perry, 1968); and Baxter Magolda's related work (Baxter Magolda, 1992) are examples of theories developed based on work with college student populations. The theories of moral development by Kohlberg (1984) and Gilligan (1993) and the intellectual development model described by Belenky, Clinchy, Goldberger and Tarule (1986) are examples of theories developed with other sample populations and found useful when applied to college students.

This chapter will examine student development theories likely to be of use, the value of the entertainment media in formal and informal teaching of those theories, and examples of entertainment media use.

Theoretical Bases of Student Development

This section provides a brief overview of developmental theories likely to be used in training paraprofessionals and students in master's-level student development theory courses. These theories address psychosocial development, cognitive structural development, and typologies. Psychosocial development is concerned with the tasks occupying individuals as they progress through the life span. Content of development (for example, the nature of developmental issues students are likely to encounter in college) is the focus. Cognitive structural development describes the structure of the meaning making that individuals use in making decisions. Typology theories "reflect individual stylistic differences in how students approach their worlds" (Evans, Forney, and Guido-DiBrito, 1998).

Psychosocial Theories. The publication of Arthur Chickering's model of the psychosocial development of college students in *Education and Identity* (Chickering, 1969) marked, for many student affairs professionals, the beginning of a body of theory applicable to their work with students. This theory, describing the life tasks often encountered by traditional-age college students, resonated with the experience of many student affairs practitioners and inspired significant research. The second edition of *Education and Identity* by Chickering and Reisser (1993) incorporated relevant research that led to some revision of the model.

The essence of this work is a theory of seven vectors of psychosocial development that details the tasks that typically occupy traditional-age undergraduate students: developing competence (in intellectual, physical, and interpersonal arenas), managing emotions, moving through autonomy toward interdependence, developing mature interpersonal relationships, establishing identity, developing purpose, and developing integrity. Environmental conditions such as an institution's size and type, articulation of and adherence to mission, and teaching styles are also factors in psychosocial development (Chickering and Reisser, 1993).

Schlossberg's transition theory (Schlossberg, Waters, and Goodman, 1995), typically categorized as a theory of adult development, is also relevant to traditional-age college students because of the many changes they are likely to experience during their college career (Evans, Forney, and Guido-DiBrito, 1998). Transitions, which are characterized by things that happen and things that are anticipated but do not occur (nonevents), have an impact on relationships, routines, assumptions, and roles. Individuals experience a process of moving in, moving through, and moving out in relation to transitions. Coping is influenced by the individual's ratio of assets and liabilities in regard to four variables: situation, self, support, and strategies (Schlossberg, Waters, and Goodman, 1995).

Cognitive Structural Theories of Intellectual Development. William Perry (1968) developed his theory of intellectual development while working with undergraduate students at Harvard in the 1950s and 1960s. Beginning with his question "Would you like to say what stands out for you during the year?" (p. 7), he elicited qualitative, longitudinal data that revealed a meaning-making structure guiding intellectual development at the majority of the positions and moral development in the most complex positions. His nine-position model reflects movement from basic dualism, in which everything is understood in black-and-white terms, with truth being absolute, to multiplicity to relativism, to the final position of developing commitment in relativism. At this final position, individuals understand who they are in terms of their life choices and resulting commitments. With this knowledge, individuals also understand the balance among these commitments.

Perry's work was a strong influence on Belenky, Clinchy, Goldberger, and Tarule, the authors of *Women's Ways of Knowing* (1986), and Marcia Baxter Magolda, author of *Knowing and Reasoning in College* (1992). Both works describe studies of intellectual development. Explicit in each study is a desire for a greater understanding of the role that gender plays in this meaning-making process. The authors of *Women's Ways of Knowing* used an all-female sample population, while Baxter Magolda used a sample population consisting of females and males and found some differences related to gender.

A qualitative study of women in both formal and informal learning environments revealed the five-perspective model described in *Women's Ways of Knowing*. As is the case with other cognitive structural theories, these perspectives—silence, received knowledge, subjective knowledge, procedural knowledge, and constructed knowledge—become increasingly complex meaning-making structures as one moves through them.

Baxter Magolda's longitudinal study of undergraduates and their ways of making meaning revealed four reasoning patterns: absolute knowing, transitional knowing, independent knowing, and contextual knowing (Baxter Magolda, 1992). These reasoning patterns are best viewed as a continuum of meaning-making structures. Baxter Magolda found these patterns to be related to but not dictated by gender. With the exception of contextual knowing, the study revealed ways of knowing within each pattern that tend to be favored by one gender.

Cognitive Structural Theories of Moral Development. Kohlberg's and Gilligan's theories of moral development were not developed specifically for use with college populations (Kohlberg, 1984; Gilligan, 1993). However, student affairs practitioners in a variety of areas find their understanding of students greatly enhanced through application of these theories. The complex questions of why students behave as they do and how they conceptualize what is good are more readily understood in the frameworks provided by Kohlberg and Gilligan.

Kohlberg's (1984) theory of moral development is organized into three levels, preconventional, conventional, and postconventional, each comprising two stages. At each stage, a different, increasingly complex reasoning process is in place. These configurations provide the structure that guides and directs individuals in the making of moral judgments. The moral structures help people understand and make sense of the world as they make those moral decisions.

In a Different Voice (1993) details Carol Gilligan's research into the way women make moral judgments. Responding, in part, to Kohlberg's finding of a predominant justice orientation in moral decision making and a resulting disregard of the care orientation more typical of women, Gilligan chose to study women in the process of making real-life moral choices rather than reacting to the hypothetical dilemmas used by Kohlberg. Her model includes three stages and two transitions that outline movement and growing complexity in moral decision making. Initially, "good" is defined as selfishness as a means of survival. Moving beyond this, an individual makes moral decisions from a frame in which responsibility to others is valued over care of the self. In the final stage, individuals understand the necessity and legitimacy of care of self being of equal importance with care of others.

Typology Theories. Typology theories enhance understanding of how individuals are both similar and different from other individuals. Understanding such theories can aid in developing an appreciation of individuals different from oneself. As Evans, Forney, and Guido-DiBrito (1998) note, typology theories can provide helpful information regarding sources of challenge and sources of support for students who differ stylistically. Prominent examples of such theories include Kolb's theory of experiential learning, which is described in Chapter One (Kolb, 1984), and Holland's theory of vocational personalities and environments (Holland, 1997).

The Relevance of Entertainment Media as Teaching Tools

Entertainment media can aid in making student development theory real for graduate students or practitioners of student development, enhancing their understanding.

From Abstraction to Reality. Graduate students often express pleasure in watching movies, listening to music, or discussing novels or plays in student development theory courses. Faculty and student affairs professionals who employ pedagogies allowing them to use these materials often comment on the effectiveness of such approaches. Students working as paraprofessionals in student affairs enjoy training that uses creative techniques that help them learn to be peer educators, orientation leaders, intramural officials, or resident assistants.

The arts allow and, in some cases, force people to experience ideas, principles, emotions, insights, and ways of being on a different level from that of intellect alone. A novel, a painting, or a song can address a concept that is difficult to express adequately in words, giving it form and substance and thus communicating its meaning (Davis, 1993). A song, verse, film, or painting, carefully chosen and discussed, can give life to the abstract concepts of student development theory, allowing students to see and understand through a different portal, a new approach to understanding.

Learning How to Observe the Articulation of Theory. Training sessions and course presentations that are thoughtfully conceived, designed, and implemented lay a solid foundation for understanding. Students listen to, view, or read a work of art and make meaning of it in a way that is relevant to the theory being applied. This process, if well facilitated, provides students with an arena in which to observe, experience, learn, understand, own, and apply complex theories. When applying theory in real-life settings, the ability to observe student behavior and ascertain the meaning making that informs the behavior is key. Using entertainment media to teach and train in this area sharpens and refines this observational skill; it also gives students material on which to practice the application of theory. Good questions by faculty, trainers, and other fellow learners guide students to the comprehension of theory they need in order to apply it.

Examples of Entertainment Media Use

Both graduate classroom instruction and undergraduate staff training are considered.

Use of Entertainment Media in a Graduate Class. Rock music can serve as a vehicle to help students make the abstract ideas of student development theory more concrete, to check students' understanding of theoretical concepts, and to introduce theories in an enjoyable, engaging manner. For several years, Dea Forney, the junior author of this chapter, has played music at the start of most classes. Students are asked at some point in the class to explain the connections between the song and the theory or theories being discussed that day. Students typically look forward to the week's musical selection. Using music provides an alternate way for the instructor to obtain awareness of students' grasp of basic theoretical ideas.

Connections between some musical selections and the corresponding theories are very evident. For example, David Bowie's "Changes" (Bowie, 1990) has an obvious link to Schlossberg's transition theory (Schlossberg,

Waters, and Goodman, 1995), and Tori Amos's "Silent All These Years" (Amos, 1991) is easily related to theorists such as Gilligan (1977) and Belenky, Clinchy, Goldberger, and Tarule (1986), who focused on women's voices. Other music requires more reflection to connect it to a particular theory or body of theory. For example, Michael W. Smith's "Place in This World" (Kirkpatrick, Grant, and Smith, 1990), which describes the challenges of establishing who one really is, can be used with a psychosocial or identity theory such as Chickering's (Chickering and Reisser, 1993). Pink's "Don't Let Me Get Me" (Pink and Austin, 2001) serves as another example of an individual struggling with issues of self and identity. Mama Cass Elliot's "Make Your Own Kind of Music" (Mann and Weil, 1999) advocates being who you are, even if you are not endorsed by others for doing so. The song can be linked to the experiences of nondominant populations such as gay, lesbian, and bisexual students and related to theories such as those of Cass (1979) and D'Augelli (1994).

The Indigo Girls' "Closer to Fine" (Saliers, 1989) and Live's "The Beauty of Gray" (Kowalczwk, Taylor, Dahlheimer, and Gracey, 1991) can stimulate connections to cognitive theories such as those of Perry (1968) and Baxter Magolda (1992). "Closer to Fine" describes a process of searching for and then rejecting absolutes, while "The Beauty of Gray" depicts the world as being more complex than black and white and promotes the value of understanding others' perspectives. Chesney Hawkes's "The One and Only" (Kershaw, 1991), perhaps better known as the theme song from the film *Doc Hollywood* (1991), promotes pride in being oneself and can be linked to typology theories such as those of Holland (1997) and Kolb (1984).

Another example of entertainment media use involves teaching Chickering and Reisser's (1993) psychosocial theory in a graduate-level student development theory course. The primary goal of this activity is an in-depth understanding of the theory. Secondary goals include the ability to recognize the theory in artistic expression and the ability to apply the theory to such expression. A final goal is that students learn to engage in dialogue leading to co-construction of knowledge. Applications such as this afford students an opportunity to work with such material and with one another in learning.

After discussing the basic tenets of the theory, seven students are randomly selected, and each is asked to draw a slip of paper from a set that has each of the seven vectors written on it. The students are not to reveal which vector they have drawn. As homework, each of these seven students is to identify a song that he or she believes illustrates the vector he or she has drawn. Each is asked to bring a visual display of the song's lyrics and a CD of the song to the following class. They are not to discuss this with their classmates prior to class.

At the beginning of the next class, the seven students play their songs and display the lyrics. There is no discussion during this process; class members are to listen and match songs and vectors. To add another level of difficulty and reality to the process, students can be asked to identify vectors simply by listening to the lyrics as the songs are played.

The final stage of the activity is processing. Beginning with the first song, class members are asked which vector they believe it represents and why. Reaching a consensus is not essential; the key is exploring what they heard and how that corresponds to what they understand this vector to be about. The students supplying the songs are asked which vector was assigned, why this song was chosen, and why it represents this vector.

Challenging students to discuss what they believe the theory to be and how they understand it in ways that have meaning for them is an important element of the activity. While students will probably do it themselves, devil's advocacy is an important aspect of the facilitation of this exercise. In order to move beyond a superficial understanding or easy agreement among class members, they need to be asked questions: "But could that mean . . . ?" "Have you thought about . . . ?" "What if you thought about it as . . . ?" Students (and faculty) also should be challenged to think about their own barriers to understanding.

The conclusion of this exercise takes the form of students articulating what they have learned and the possibilities for application of their learning. Depending on class size, learning styles, and time constraints, this portion of the exercise can be completed with the entire class, in journals, or in small groups. The process is incomplete if students do not articulate what they learned, how they understand this theory, and how they can apply it in a student affairs setting. Putting the theory in their own words helps them own the material. Being able to articulate it to another student or a faculty member, either orally or in writing, forces them to be able to understand it well enough to explain it.

Like songs, movies can easily illustrate the theories outlined here. Examples include using *Finding Nemo* (2003) and *St. Elmo's Fire* (1985) to show characters facing the psychosocial challenges detailed in Chickering and Reisser (1993). Moral reasoning and the structures in which it occurs are clearly visible in *To Kill a Mockingbird* (1962), *A Time to Kill* (1996), and *A Few Good Men* (1992); these films vividly bring Kohlberg's stages (Kohlberg, 1984) to life. *The Joy Luck Club* (1993) and *Thelma and Louise* (1991) provide students a multitude of scenarios for the application of Gilligan's theory of moral development (Gilligan, 1993). *Sense and Sensibility* (1995), *Sleeping with the Enemy* (1991), and *9 to 5* (1980) all illustrate the positions emerging from Belenky, Clinchy, Goldberger, and Tarule's study as explained in *Women's Ways of Knowing* (Belenky, Clinchy, Goldberger, and Tarule, 1986). William Perry's positions (Perry, 1968) are evident in *Dead Poets Society* (1989) and *Good Will Hunting* (1997).

Use of Entertainment Media in Training. Paraprofessional staff training in a variety of settings, such as multicultural centers, counseling centers, student programming offices, and residence halls, provides another opportunity to use student development theory as a foundation for the work done by students with and for their fellow students. As with graduate students, the more engaged the trainees are with the material, the more likely they are to retain and ultimately use what they have learned.

Using a film as a theme for training is one way to connect a variety of training components while encouraging students to think creatively about their work. A film can also be a creative and engaging vehicle for a process that can be lengthy, tiring, and tedious. Goals for such training would be to expose undergraduate staff members to the content, purposes, uses, and application of developmental theory in their work in student affairs. Use of one film allows themes to be elaborated and reinforced repeatedly, increasing the chances of retention and use. Using a classic, current, or appealing film enhances the likelihood of students embracing this method. Classic movies become cultural reference points, and current popular movies provide a common experience and understanding.

For these reasons, the film *Casablanca* (1942) is a good choice. Many people are familiar with this film and have clear images of it; however, there are a number of significant themes in it that may not be casually remembered. Set during World War II, the film is a love story lived within the morally complex context of war. Rick, an allegedly apolitical bar owner; Ilsa, his former lover; and her husband, Victor Lazslo, come together in Nazi-occupied Casablanca. There, in a brief period of time, they work to understand and make decisions related to the universal themes of love, loyalty, commitment, betrayal, and living out their most deeply held, often competing beliefs. All of this takes place within their interwoven and not-completely-understood relationships.

The first step is to have all staff members watch the film together, to ensure that everyone has the same information and experience. This experience could be part of a significant event such as a training kickoff. *Casablanca* provides a number of useful themes, including making choices; issues of care and justice; ethics (especially in situations and structures that are beyond individual control); stereotypes; courage; and political realities. An overarching theme could be "Making Choices," with a subtitle of "What We Did for Love." Given the place of this film in our collective memory, the possibilities for creative session titles are endless.

A session on applications of Gilligan's and Kohlberg's theories could begin by identifying all the moral decisions in this film. Examples include Ilsa's indecision and decision about where she belongs and Rick's role in Victor and Ilsa leaving Casablanca. This identification could lead to a discussion of what moral decision making may be involved in the roles of the staff members. What do they need to think about prior to the point of having to make these decisions? What do they believe their structures of meaning making to be? Discussing these issues in terms of movie characters may make it easier for staff members to see the issues in their own situation. Ethical decision making within confining and distinct contexts could also be discussed; *Casablanca* provides an abundance of examples, and this exploration could facilitate a discussion of the influences of environments on development.

Working toward an enhanced understanding of group dynamics could involve a discussion of the differences between care and justice orientations and how they affect the approach that group members take in relating to one another and in problem solving. Such a session could also include information about intellectual development and how that reveals itself in group settings and in how students learn, both in and outside of the classroom.

Because *Casablanca* portrays a distinct environment with strongly competing forces, it also provides a good opening for discussion of person-environment interaction as a developmental process and a means to understanding behavior. Such an exercise could be useful for environments as diverse as student unions, offices serving underrepresented populations, recreation facilities, dining halls, and residence halls.

Assignments. Assignments that use a variety of entertainment media allow students to expand on techniques and skills of application learned in class. Possibilities include analysis of a work of art (prose, poetry, painting, sculpture, song lyric, or film) from the perspective of one or more of the theorists studied. Students could take a character from fiction (a film, book, or play) and apply one or more of the theories studied in order to better understand their character and his or her actions.

Conclusion

Here is one caution for those using entertainment media: remember that the theory has to be central and has to be well understood on its own, through the words of the authors revealing it and the words of those critiquing, applying, and elaborating on it. Once we and our students have that level of understanding, these theories can become ours. As educators working from a student affairs orientation, we tend to think of learning as play and fun, or at least, we have that as a goal. As educators, we also strive to make theory live and breathe because we understand how crucial that is in a practice-based field. Perhaps that is why so many of us are drawn to using entertainment media to teach and train students. As this sourcebook illustrates, there are a multitude of ways to use media in pursuit of these goals.

References

Amos, T. "Silent All These Years." CD, *Little Earthquakes*. United States: Atlantic Recording Corporation, 1991.

Baxter Magolda, M. B. *Knowing and Reasoning in College: Gender-Related Patterns in Students' Intellectual Development*. San Francisco: Jossey-Bass, 1992.

Belenky, M. F., Clinchy, B. M., Goldberger, N. R., and Tarule, J. M. *Women's Ways of Knowing: The Development of Self, Voice and Mind*. New York: Basic Books, 1986.

Bowie, D. "Changes." CD, *Changesbowie*. United Kingdom: EMI Records, 1990 (recorded 1971).

Casablanca [motion picture]. United States: Warner Brothers, 1942.

Cass, V. C. "Homosexual Identity Formation: A Theoretical Model." *Journal of Homosexuality*, 1979, 4(3), 219–235.

Chickering, A. W. *Education and Identity*. San Francisco: Jossey-Bass, 1969.

Chickering, A. W., and Reisser, L. *Education and Identity*. (2nd ed.) San Francisco: Jossey-Bass, 1993.

D'Augelli, A. R. "Identity Development and Sexual Orientation: Toward a Model of Lesbian, Gay, and Bisexual Development." In E. J. Trickett, R. J. Watts, and D. Birman (eds.), *Human Diversity: Perspectives on People in Context*. San Francisco: Jossey-Bass, 1994.

Davis, B. G. *Tools for Teaching*. San Francisco: Jossey-Bass, 1993.

Dead Poets Society [motion picture]. United States: Touchstone Video, 1989.

Doc Hollywood [motion picture]. United States: Warner Brothers, 1991.

Evans, N. K., Forney, D. S., and Guido-DiBrito, F. *Student Development in College: Theory, Research, and Practice*. San Francisco: Jossey-Bass, 1998.

A Few Good Men [motion picture]. United States: Columbia/Tri-Star, 1992.

Finding Nemo [motion picture]. United States: Walt Disney Home Video, 2003.

Gilligan, C. "In a Different Voice: Women's Conceptions of Self and Morality." *Harvard Education Review*, 1977, 47(4), 481–517.

Gilligan, C. *In a Different Voice: Psychological Theory and Women's Development*. Cambridge, Mass.: Harvard University Press, 1993.

Good Will Hunting [motion picture]. United States: Miramax Films, 1997.

Holland, J. L. *Making Vocational Choices: A Theory of Vocational Personalities and Work Environments*. (3rd ed.) Odessa, FL: Psychological Assessment Resources, 1997.

The Joy Luck Club [motion picture]. United States: Buena Vista Home Entertainment, 1993.

Kershaw, N. "The One and Only." [Recorded by Chesney Hawkes]. CD, *The One and Only*. United States: Chrysalis Records, 1991.

Kirkpatrick, W., Grant, A., and Smith, M. W. "Place in This World." [Recorded by Michael W. Smith]. CD, *Go West Young Man*. United States: RCA Records, 1990.

Kohlberg, L. *Essays on Moral Development, Vol. 2: The Psychology of Moral Development: The Nature and Validity of Moral Stages*. New York: HarperCollins, 1984.

Kolb, D. A. *Experiential Learning: Experience as the Source of Learning and Development*. Englewood Cliffs, N.J.: Prentice Hall, 1984.

Kowalczwk, E., Taylor, C., Dahlheimer, P., and Gracey, C. "The Beauty of Gray." [Recorded by Live]. CD, *Mental Jewelry*. United States: MCA Records, 1991.

Mann, B., and Weil, C. "Make Your Own Kind of Music." [Recorded by Cass Elliott]. CD, *The Best of the Mamas and the Papas: 20th Century Masters The Millennium Collection*. United States: MCA Records, 1999 (recorded 1969).

9 to 5 [motion picture]. United States: Twentieth Century Fox, 1980.

Perry, W. G., Jr. *Forms of Intellectual and Ethical Development in the College Years: A Scheme*. New York: Holt, Rinehart and Winston, 1968.

Pink and Austin, D. "Don't Let Me Get Me." [Recorded by Pink]. CD, *Missundaztood*. United States: Arista Records, 2001.

St. Elmo's Fire [motion picture]. United States: Columbia/Tri-Star, 1985.

Saliers, E. "Closer to Fine." [Recorded by Indigo Girls]. CD, *Indigo Girls*. United States: CBS Records, 1989.

Schlossberg, N. K., Waters, E. B., and Goodman, J. *Counseling Adults in Transition*. (2nd ed.) New York: Springer, 1995.

Sense and Sensibility [motion picture]. United States: Columbia/Tri-Star, 1995.

Sleeping with the Enemy [motion picture]. United States: Twentieth Century Fox, 1991.

"The Student Personnel Point of View, 1937." In G. L. Saddlemire and A. L. Rentz (eds.), *Student Affairs—A Profession's Heritage*. Washington, D.C.: American College Personnel Association, 1983.

Thelma and Louise [motion picture]. United States: MGM/UA Studios, 1991.
A Time to Kill [motion picture]. United States: Warner Brothers, 1996.
To Kill a Mockingbird [motion picture]. United States: Universal Studios, 1962.

Merrily S. Dunn is assistant professor and program coordinator of the College Student Affairs Administration Program in the Department of Counseling and Human Development Services at the University of Georgia in Athens.

Deanna S. Forney is professor of college student personnel in the Department of Educational and Interdisciplinary Studies at Western Illinois University in Macomb, Illinois.

3

This chapter discusses the importance of enhancing the diversity awareness and multicultural competence of undergraduate and graduate students through the use of popular media for classes and training workshops, and it presents two models that explain behaviors associated with racial identity development and understanding diversity issues.

Using Entertainment Media to Inform Student Affairs Teaching and Practice About Multiculturalism

Mary F. Howard-Hamilton, Kandace G. Hinton

It is important that student affairs administrators and faculty encourage undergraduate and graduate students to become multiculturally competent and sensitive to diversity issues. As our society becomes more racially and ethnically diverse, we need to include images that reflect the changing demographics. Moreover, these images should be empowering, nondiscriminatory, and truthful. The media have transmitted information that can be biased, particularly when one negative theme is reiterated over a long period of time. Television has portrayed nonwhite racial and ethnic groups as culturally inferior and subservient to white middle-class society since its inception nearly seventy years ago (Staples and Jones, 1995). Furthermore, television and film continue to perpetuate the racial ideology that persons from minority groups are second-class citizens. For example, the presentation of American Indians as savages, Mexicans as lazy, Asians as sly and sinister, or African Americans as drug dealers and pimps has consigned these groups to stereotypical roles. Much of what Americans know about diverse groups has been learned from biased accounts or inaccurate portrayals of people of color while viewing popular television programming, the news, or film as well as listening to talk radio. However, the media can also educate and reduce prejudices if material is selected that can evoke enough cognitive dissonance to challenge old assumptions and prejudices in order to make way for transformative thought.

Cortes (2000) notes that in our society, the four forms of curriculum that inform how we view our world, ourselves, and others are (1) the immediate curriculum—the people we have the deepest and most profound communication with on a daily basis; (2) the institutional curriculum—our schools, churches, and workplaces; (3) the serendipitous curriculum—people who are part of our lives by chance or situations that do not occur on a regular basis; and (4) the media curriculum—what we read in the newspapers and books, what we see on television, and what we hear on the radio. Cortes (2000, p. 55) says that the media produce five types of multicultural content:

1. Media present information about individual groups and broader multicultural topics.
2. Media organize information and ideas about constituent societal groups and other aspects of diversity.
3. Media disseminate values about groups, intergroup relations, other dimensions of multiculturalism, and diversity itself.
4. Media address audience expectations about diversity, including specific topics and groups.
5. Media provide models of behavior for members of individual groups, for the treatment of members of other groups, and for ways of dealing with diversity.

Students watch television shows that reflect their own racial or ethnic group (Berk, 2002). During the 2001–2002 television season, white people watched situation comedies that had no nonwhite racial or ethnic groups in the casts such as *Everybody Loves Raymond, Friends, Will and Grace, Frasier,* and *Just Shoot Me.* Hispanic/Latino households watched Univision (the Spanish network) primarily. African Americans watched situation comedies with predominantly black casts, such as *The Bernie Mac Show, My Wife and Kids,* and *The Hughleys.* Berk noted that "in general, TV viewing appears to be an ethnically segregated experience" (2002, p. 83). This information is extremely disconcerting, since our society comprises diverse individuals, and if many students are taking their cultural and communicative cues from segregated situation comedies, how will this phenomenon influence intergroup, intragroup, and interpersonal perceptions (Cortes, 2000)? Racial identity models can assist student affairs practitioners and students in understanding the levels of comfort and discomfort a person feels when dealing with diversity issues. Furthermore, understanding and using racial identity models can help in the development of workshops and programs as well as provide a comfortable place to begin a dialogue about diversity.

White Racial Identity Development

If students are to become open-minded about issues related to diversity, the first step is for them to be comfortable with the idea that everyone is a racial being. This concept is difficult to accept for a large number of white people because they rarely think of themselves in terms of a color or race; they think of themselves as a human or an American. When students who have not been socialized to accept and embrace diversity are introduced to multicultural media, they may have some initial resistance. Thus, understanding how white people develop racial identity is critical to preparing workshop or course materials that are sequenced in a manner that is cognitively challenging but not too much of a stretch from students' current mode of thinking. In developmental terminology, this is called "plus one" staging (Kohlberg, 1984)— that is, introducing topics that are one step or stage above the current level of cognitive development.

Helms and Cook (1999) provide an overview of white racial identity and note that there are seven statuses in the model: Contact, Disintegration, Reintegration, Pseudo-Independence, Immersion, Emersion, and Autonomy. Each status represents different behaviors and levels of discomfort or comfort when engaging with diversity issues.

In Contact status, whites are not aware of who they are as racial beings. Furthermore, they embrace the status quo and believe that there is balance among racial groups in our society. As whites explore their identity, they are shocked and surprised to learn about unearned group privileges (Evans, Forney, and Guido-DiBrito, 1998).

Disintegration involves becoming aware of the moral dilemmas of race in the United States and becoming aware of one's own whiteness, with confusion resulting. To reduce the bewilderment about racial groups and develop new beliefs as individuals enter Reintegration status, whites adopt beliefs reflecting the idea that whites are superior to those of other racial or ethnic groups. "A person can stay in Reintegration until a jarring event causes abandonment of a racist identity" (Evans, Forney, and Guido-DiBrito, 1998, p. 78). As white people begin to question and challenge the definition of whiteness and the justification for different modes of racism, they enter Pseudo-Independence status.

"The Pseudo-Independence status is characterized by an intellectualized commitment to one's racial group in which one identifies with the 'good' nonracist Whites and rejects the 'bad' racists" (Helms and Cook, 1999, p. 92). Once the "good" and the "bad" people have been identified, the Immersion process involves a search for honest and accurate information about race and racism, including a "non-racist definition of Whiteness" (Helms and Cook, 1999, p. 92). Once such a definition has been cognitively and emotionally processed, the Emersion status finds the person working with a community of reeducated white people who are seeking new information about diversity. In the last status, Autonomy, there is a connection to one's racial community, understanding of the complexity of diversity and multiculturalism, and an ability to reject or challenge socialized stereotypes and renounce the privileges of racism.

Development and growth of white racial identity can be facilitated by introducing documentary or popular films, television shows, or music about diverse populations that provide stimulating images as well as examples of oppression and white privilege. However, the use of multicultural media should be appropriately staged, for if the information introduced is beyond students' psychosocial and cognitive level of development, they may close their mind to the material and retreat into their original comfortable or privileged position.

Understanding other racial identity development models can also assist in facilitating multicultural class discussions and workshop sessions that are representative of a diverse audience or population. Some examples are the Nigrescence Model for Black Identity Development (Cross, 1995; Cross and Vandiver, 2001); the Hispanic Bicultural Identity Model (Torres, 1999); the Asian American Identity Development Model (Kim, 2001); the Minority Identity Development Model (Atkinson, Morten, and Sue, 1998); the African American Resistance Model (Robinson and Howard-Hamilton, 2000), and the Multiracial Identity Development Model (Poston, 1990).

Multicultural Competence

A culturally competent student (Howard-Hamilton, Richardson, and Shuford, 1998) is one who appreciates the inclusion of diversity topics in the curriculum and programming. Furthermore, culturally competent students can walk the walk and talk the talk about diversity comfortably without fear of being ostracized by their own counterparts and can respond when they see injustices taking place. Overall, these students appreciate who they are as racial and ethnic individuals and also appreciate cultures both similar to and different from their own group. There is continual self-reflection and understanding that being different is acceptable. Cognitively, culturally competent students have a desire to learn about issues of oppression and how these affect society as well as themselves personally. They have an understanding of the complexity of multiple identities and the intersections of race, gender, socioeconomic status, lifestyle, and religion. Accordingly, they can connect with people from multiple perspectives and understand from a moral stance that it is unjust to discriminate based on immutable characteristics or cultural variables.

The greatest challenge for culturally competent students is to step forward when acts of discrimination are taking place, to communicate their displeasure and discomfort with the situation and take a risk to change what has occurred. This challenge involves a willingness to become involved in social change that may create a complete shift in whom the student associates with on a daily basis. At this intersection, our role as educators and administrators is to model the way for these students (Howard-Hamilton, Richardson, and Shuford, 1998).

Creative teaching practices have helped students make transitions through complex behaviors when attempting to make adjustments to their belief system about diversity issues. We, the authors of this chapter, have taught a class on diversity issues in graduate preparation programs at three separate institutions for more than eight years. We have observed the behaviors students exhibit in class, reviewed comments written in their journals, noted their conversations in class, and documented personal meetings. From these observations, we have developed a model based on five common behavioral themes that surfaced when students began and ended their experience during the sixteen weeks in class.

The Howard-Hamilton and Hinton Model for Diversity Awareness and Multicultural Competence is cyclical, because students will recycle or rotate through the model continually as new information or stimuli are introduced that create some form of healthy dissonance (Torres, Howard-Hamilton, and Cooper, 2003). The cyclical nature of the behaviors in the model are shown in Figure 3.1.

The first theme is anticipatory anxiety in which students exhibit a sense of positive anxiousness or normal anxiety about the course and the things that they will be learning. They have opened their minds and want to delve into the topics planned for the semester, to learn more about themselves and multicultural groups. Some students are not excited about the course or the content, and they exhibit a tremendous amount of anxiety about how others view their culture. Some of the overall feelings at the beginning of

Figure 3.1. Behavioral Patterns in the Howard-Hamilton and Hinton Model for Diversity Awareness and Multicultural Competence

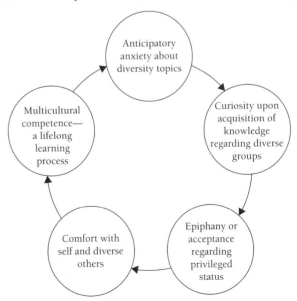

Source: Adapted from Torres, Howard-Hamilton, and Cooper, *Identity Development of Diverse Populations.* Copyright © 2003 by Wiley Periodicals, Inc. This material is used by permission of John Wiley & Sons, Inc.

the term are excitement, hopefulness, joy, and openness. At the opposite end of the continuum are other feelings of anxiety, anger, frustration, fear, guilt, and shame. When individuals must move from the known to the unknown, they experience varying forms of anxiety (Corey, 2001). If students take a risk and use the freedom that they have to listen to the subtle message of anxiety, the direction of their lives may change.

Students who start to open their minds and yield to the anxiety become curious upon acquiring new knowledge about multiculturalism and diversity. At first, they are shocked and appalled when they discover that there is so much to learn about the history of diverse groups, and that their current level of education is woefully inadequate. They have a desire and readiness to read and learn more about the history of culturally diverse people.

Once they have read varying versions of the history and treatment of multicultural groups in this country, some students may realize that they have been the beneficiaries of unearned privileges. The next theme, epiphany or acceptance regarding privileged status, involves the students' recognition of how pervasive privilege is in our society and how many of them have covertly or overtly used these benefits without questioning how or why this power was acquired. It should be noted that the classes are racially and ethnically diverse, and even the Latino and black students recognize that certain unearned privileges apply to them as well, such as classism, gender, or able-bodiedness. Overall, they begin to understand how history can be shaped to erase the contributions of oppressed groups, and the new knowledge empowers them to search for information that was not biased or altered, or that did not marginalize the contributions of underrepresented groups in America.

The fourth theme is comfort with self and others. Following the epiphany, it is important for individuals to embrace their racial, ethnic, or cultural heritages so that they have personal peace and empathy for those who also have a cultural connection with meaningful stories. The best way for students to understand themselves is to reflect on their own racial and ethnic identities. This is accomplished through writing about themselves and making a connection with how their families, friends, church, communities, and the media, to name just a few, influenced their beliefs and behaviors about multicultural groups. The stories are written in a personal journal, and it is important for the students to make a connection whenever possible with the lecture, readings, films, or discussions from class. Students may also make a meaningful connection between the classroom materials and what they experience on campus or in their home environments.

Many students who experience an emotionally challenging situation may not feel as though they can tell their stories to others who do not have the capacity or multicultural competence to understand what they have encountered. The fourth theme, comfort with self and others, allows the individual to empathize and be open to learning more about the other person or situation. In each class, students are asked to share a meaningful story from their journals. This prepares others to become comfortable with the different and often unpleasant scenarios that occur on a daily basis on campus or in a person's home environment.

These multicultural stories will be shared, and the learning process will continue for everyone; multicultural competence becomes a lifelong endeavor, as noted in the final theme. The students have a sense of social consciousness and personal passion to continue the fight against oppression. The students will need to maintain a level of normal anxiety and continue to be willing to connect with others not like themselves, to examine the role of privilege in their lives, and to increase their knowledge base so that they expand their multicultural competence and enhance their level of racial identity development.

The use of entertainment media in classes and workshops provides students with the opportunity to view the lives of others in a safe environment and to discuss and interpret the information with a facilitator or faculty member, along with classmates or fellow workshop participants. This type of information sharing helps students become multiculturally competent by exposing them to information that subverts the hidden stereotypical agenda that is often packaged by the popular media, either consciously or unconsciously.

The Use of Entertainment Media in the Classroom and Training

Graduate and undergraduate classrooms and training workshops receive attention in the following sections.

Using Entertainment Media in Classroom Instruction. Entertainment media can be used to evoke healthy cognitive dissonance and challenge preconceived stereotypes, biases, and prejudices about racial and ethnic groups and multicultural populations. Numerous films, television shows, books, and pieces of music have been produced that highlight hegemonic, racial, and ethnic themes. A movie can be used as an assessment tool to determine how well students in a graduate preparation course on diversity issues have understood the readings and theoretical frameworks and how well they can apply them. We selected the movie *Places in the Heart* (1984) for this purpose.

In the film, Edna Spalding is a woman who has been recently widowed and who suddenly has to figure out how to support herself and her two children during the Depression. Moze, a black man looking for room and board, offers the suggestion of growing cotton and, desperate to try anything that will keep her family together, Spalding accepts his assistance. More important than Edna's need for money is proving to the white men in her small town that she can survive without patriarchal help. Her life experiences up to then had been those of a wife and a mother, and nothing more had been asked of her. A blind boarder, Mr. Will, "sees" the harshness and bigotries of life and is a quiet yet interesting observer of what's going on around him. Added to this mix are Edna's brother-in-law Wayne and sister Margaret, who go through marital struggles when Wayne becomes involved with another woman. They fight the basic human problem of being a good person but making bad decisions.

Places in the Heart is a realistic look at the lives and views of people in the 1930s. The film tackles issues such as racism, sexism, privilege, oppression, ableism, classism, spirituality, and people learning to live again after they've had to overcome many obstacles. We developed a midterm exam based on the issues in the film.

Our students were to view the movie using their newly constructed multicultural lenses. Using a multicultural perspective helps white and nonwhite students advance their understanding of white privilege and racial inequality and assists in the exploration and deconstruction of white racial identity (Ortiz and Rhoads, 2000). Students were given two weeks to view the film. They were asked to provide narrative responses to the exam questions and to make use of the assigned readings to support their responses. Following are a few examples of the exam questions:

What lessons took place in the film that can be applied to today's college student population and the campus environment?

How were Mrs. Spalding's children (Possum and Frank) affected by the people and events in their lives? (Use a racial identity model for each child, and discuss their development from the beginning to the end of the film.)

Discuss Mrs. Spalding, Moses, and Mr. Will within the context of race, gender, disability, socioeconomic status, and culture.

Discuss Mrs. Spalding's ethnic, racial, and womanist identity development throughout the film.

What does the movie say to you about the social construction of race, gender, disability, and class during the 1930s, and how does this compare and contrast with race, gender, and class discourses in the twenty-first century?

How was empowerment facilitated throughout this film?

Using Entertainment Media in Training Workshops. *Places in the Heart* (1984) can also be used in a workshop setting. For example, students can be divided into small groups and asked to discuss the various forms of oppression and privilege shown in the film. Prior to showing the film, it is important for a facilitator to explain how to observe and recognize these forms of discrimination.

During a training workshop, several identity development models may be presented, but theoretical information and other material may be truncated as needed to fit into the compressed timeframe of a workshop. Little time may be available to fully explain and evaluate each participant's level of identity development. Barker-Hackett and Mio (2000, p. 110) find that it is "best if one quickly presents these models, then divides the audience into groups of 8–10 people to discuss how" the themes, stages, and statuses connect to their lives.

After presenting and processing the identity development and behavioral diversity awareness models, *Higher Learning* (1995), a diversity film, can be used to assess the competence and awareness goals for the workshop. In this film, students are faced with conflicts over multiculturalism, sexual orientation, heterosexism, racial tension, rape, responsibility, and the meaning of an education on a university campus. The setting is fictional Columbus University; into this place of higher learning comes a mix of students to join the already multicultural pot. Malik is a black track star who feels he is disadvantaged because he has to train for track and study, while others only have to study. Remy is a white teenager who is forced out of his dorm by his black roommate and finds friendship in an extreme group. Kristen is a young female who struggles to make friends and is assaulted by a man before falling in with a women's group.

As Seyforth and Golde (2001) point out, Professor Maurice Epps tries to push the cognitive limits and promote the intellectual development of the students in his class. He states: "Life, liberty, and the pursuit of happiness. Despite having these rights, very few people exercise them. It is that kind of apathy that corrodes our society from within. Your assignment this semester is as follows: to formulate your own political ideology. This will be dictated by your sex, background, socioeconomic status, personal experiences, et cetera, et cetera. This course will be like anything in life—it will be what you make of it" (*Higher Learning,* 1995, cited in Seyforth and Golde, 2001, p. 5).

After the participants view *Higher Learning,* they are asked to write for two to three minutes to answer the question "What were your reactions to and how did you feel about what you saw in the film?" After they have written their thoughts, we place them into same-race dyads to discuss how they felt. Same-race dyads allow students the opportunity to express emotions and thoughts comfortably with peers who can empathize with the difficulty of processing segments of a movie that evoke tension and distress. The students are told that each person can share her or his feelings and thoughts for two minutes and the other person must listen.

Once each person has shared her or his thoughts and while they are still in dyads, the students can engage in an open conversation for five minutes. The entire group is brought together for a discussion of thoughts and feelings about the film. This can be facilitated by having the persons of color share their thoughts first and then having the white students share their impressions, or vice versa. It is important that everyone listens intently to what is said. The facilitator summarizes what has been heard and connects the film with the theories once again, so that the participants can see how racial identity development can affect an individual's sensitivity to diversity issues and communication with persons from other cultures.

Conclusion

Using entertainment media allows individuals to step inside the shoes of another person or immerse themselves in another culture in a safe fashion, without the high risk of failing. Films can catch individuals' attention quickly and leave little to the imagination (Seyforth and Golde, 2001). Individuals have an opportunity to experience people, places, and things that may not ever appear in their lives. "Media reportage . . . can promote attitudes of acceptance or of hostility and fear. It can expose problems and present suggested solutions or it can ignore uncomfortable situations until they explode" (Gomes and Williams, 1995, p. 345). Using appropriate multicultural media helps to create a positive image of people who have often been subconsciously judged as deficient. "People may not realize that they have prejudices, including media-fostered prejudices, about a certain group until they encounter individuals from that group or are exposed to a media barrage about that group" (Cortes, 2001, p. 179). Classes, programs, and workshops that present theory intertwined with positive media images can foster a shift in attitudes toward diverse groups as well as enhance the presenter's own level of multicultural competence.

References

Atkinson, D. R., Morten, G., and Sue, D. W. *Counseling American Minorities.* (5th ed.) San Francisco: McGraw-Hill, 1998.

Barker-Hackett, L., and Mio, J. S. "Addressing Resistance in Large Groups." In J. S. Mio and G. I. Awakuni (eds.), *Resistance to Multiculturalism: Issues and Interventions.* Philadelphia: Brunner/Mazel, 2000.

Berk, R. A. *Humor as an Instructional Defibrillator.* Sterling, VA: Stylus Press, 2002.

Corey, G. *Theory and Practice of Counseling and Psychology.* (6th ed.) Belmont, CA: Brooks/Cole, 2001.

Cortes, C. E. *The Children Are Watching: How the Media Teach About Diversity.* New York: Teachers College Press, 2000.

Cortes, C. E. "Knowledge Construction and Popular Culture: The Media as Multicultural Educator." In J. A. Banks and C. A. McGee-Banks (eds.), *Handbook of Research on Multicultural Education.* San Francisco: Jossey-Bass, 2001.

Cross, W. E. "The Psychology of Nigrescence: Revising the Cross Model." In J. G. Ponterotto, J. M. Casas, L. A. Suzuki, and C. M. Alexander (eds.), *Handbook of Multicultural Counseling.* Thousand Oaks, CA: Sage, 1995.

Cross, W. E., and Vandiver, B. J. "Nigrescence Theory and Measurement: Introducing the Cross Racial Identity Scale (CRIS)." In J. G. Ponterotto, J. M. Casas, L. A. Suzuki, and C. M. Alexander (eds.), *Handbook of Multicultural Counseling.* (2nd ed.) Thousand Oaks, CA: Sage, 2001.

Evans, N. J., Forney, D. S., and Guido-DiBrito, F. *Student Development in College: Theory, Research, and Practice.* San Francisco: Jossey-Bass, 1998.

Gomes, R. C., and Williams, L. F. "Race and Crime: The Role of the Media in Perpetuating Racism and Classism in America." In A. Aguirre and D. V. Baker (eds.), *Sources: Notable Selections in Race and Ethnicity.* Guilford, CT: Dushkin Publishing Group, 1995.

Helms, J. E., and Cook, D. A. *Using Race and Culture in Counseling and Psychotherapy: Theory and Process.* Needham Heights, MA: Allyn & Bacon, 1999.

Higher Learning [motion picture]. United States: Columbia Pictures, 1995.

Howard-Hamilton, M. F., Richardson, B. J., and Shuford, B. "Promoting Multicultural Education: A Holistic Approach." *College Student Affairs Journal,* 1998, *18*(1), 5–17.

Kim, J. "Asian American Identity Development Theory." In C. L. Wijeyesinghe and B. W. Jackson III (eds.), *New Perspectives on Racial Identity Development: A Theoretical and Practical Anthology.* New York: New York University Press, 2001.

Kohlberg, L. *Essays on Moral Development,* Vol. 2: *The Psychology of Moral Development: The Nature and Validity of Moral Stages.* New York: HarperCollins, 1984.

Ortiz, A. M., and Rhoads, R. A. "Deconstructing Whiteness as Part of a Multicultural Framework: From Theory to Practice." *Journal of College Student Development,* 2000, *41*(1), 81–93.

Places in the Heart [motion picture] United States: Fox Home Entertainment (TriStar Pictures), 1984.

Poston, W.S.C. "The Biracial Identity Development Model: A Needed Addition." *Journal of Counseling and Development,* 1990, *69*(2), 152–155.

Robinson, T. L., and Howard-Hamilton, M. F. *The Convergence of Race, Ethnicity, and Gender: Multiple Identities in Counseling.* Columbus, OH: Merrill, 2000.

Seyforth, S. C., and Golde, C. M. "Beyond *The Paper Chase:* Using Movies to Help Students Get More Out of College." *About Campus,* 2001, *6*(4), 2–9.

Staples, R., and Jones, T. "Culture, Ideology and Black Television Images." In A. Aguirre and D. V. Baker (eds.), *Sources: Notable Selections in Race and Ethnicity.* Guilford, CT: Dushkin Publishing Group, 1995.

Torres, V. "Validation of a Bicultural Orientation Model for Hispanic College Students." *Journal of College Student Development,* 1999, *40*(3), 285–299.

Torres, V., Howard-Hamilton, M. F., and Cooper, D. L. *Identity Development of Diverse Populations: Implications for Teaching and Administration in Higher Education.* ASHE Higher Education Report, vol. 29, no. 6. San Francisco: Jossey-Bass, 2003.

MARY F. HOWARD-HAMILTON is associate dean of graduate studies in the School of Education and associate professor in the Department of Educational Leadership and Policy Studies, Higher Education and Student Affairs Program at Indiana University Bloomington.

KANDACE G. HINTON is assistant professor in the Department of Educational Leadership, Administration, and Foundations, Higher Education and Leadership Program at Indiana State University–Terre Haute.

This chapter presents theoretical foundations, resources, and entertainment media applications for working with lesbian, gay, bisexual, and transgender (LGBT) undergraduate and graduate students.

Using Entertainment Media to Inform Student Affairs Teaching and Practice Related to Sexual Orientation

Tony W. Cawthon

The presence of lesbian, gay, bisexual, and transgender (LGBT) individuals within society varies greatly, due to many factors. The size, environment, history, and nature of a community affect this visibility. The higher education community is similar in that the awareness of LGBT students varies greatly from campus to campus. As in society, factors such as campus size, history, and cultural climate affect how noticeable these students are in the daily functioning of our campus communities.

Regardless of the degree of visibility of campus LGBT students, in recent years, our society has seen significant increases in attention to LGBT individuals and their issues, and this increased attention is reflected in our culture. Television shows such as *Will and Grace, The L Word,* and *Queer as Folk* feature lead characters that are gay or lesbian, and shows such as *Six Feet Under, Dawson's Creek,* and *Buffy the Vampire Slayer* feature gay or lesbian recurring characters. Likewise, films such as *Kissing Jessica Stein; The Adventures of Priscilla, Queen of the Desert;* and *Boys on the Side* portray gay or lesbian lead or secondary characters. As gay television networks evolve and gay and lesbian film festivals gain prominence, advertisers specifically target the LGBT community. Sports figures such as Martina Navratilova, Billy Bean, and Esera Tuaolo serve as role models for aspiring athletes. Organizations such as the Human Rights Campaign and the National Gay and Lesbian Task Force advocate for LGBT civil liberties, and courts are dealing with the legal issues of domestic partnership, sodomy laws, and gay adoption (Walters, 2001).

LGBT Language and Terminology

Regardless of the degree of visibility of the LGBT community on each campus, this population exists on all college and university campuses. Student affairs professionals are often called on to provide support, programming, and resources for LGBT students and their allies.

A source of confusion that student affairs professionals must contend with stems from the multitude of terms used when referring to the LGBT population. These terms serve as a source of inaccuracies. Individuals not familiar with this population are quick to use words like *gay, lesbian, sexual identity,* and *homosexual* interchangeably, when in reality, they have distinct meanings.

Significant confusion is associated with the terms *sexual identity* and *gender identity.* The concept of sexual identity (Barret and Logan, 2002) reflects an increasing acknowledgment of the impact that sexual feelings and behavior have on one's perception of self. Ryan and Futterman (1998) identify three types of identity: gender identity, sex roles identity, and sexual orientation identity. They state that gender identity reflects whether one identifies as male or female and may or may not mirror one's biological sex, and that sex roles are those positions and judgments one learns at an early age about male and female behaviors. Sexual orientation identity applies to the feelings and behaviors an individual maintains for others of the same sex (homosexuality), opposite sex (heterosexuality), or both sexes (bisexuality) (Barret and Logan, 2002).

The term *queer* originally meant "odd" but acquired a sexual connotation in the twentieth century (Stewart, 1995). Like the term *homosexual, queer* was an offensive term; however, with the growth of the lesbian and gay movement, many young LGBT individuals have embraced this word for personal identity expression (Sanlo, 1998; Stewart, 1995). Despite this confusion, the most commonly accepted current terms are *gay men* and *lesbians.*

The word *bisexual* (those attracted to both biological sexes) was not given much credibility until the work of Kinsey, who identified it as a distinct identity (Stewart, 1995). Bisexuality is difficult to define and is variously defined as a personal identity, a behavior or desire, and a state of being (Morrow, 1989).

Also often misunderstood is the term *transgender.* Transgendered individuals may be heterosexual, homosexual, bisexual, or asexual; transgender refers to an array of gender-nonconforming identities. Included in these nonconforming identities are gender benders, transvestites, and transsexuals (Ryan and Futterman, 1998).

Because many students begin dealing with their sexuality in college, student affairs practitioners also need an understanding of the term *coming out. Coming out* generally refers to a process, not an isolated event. It is the process of identifying oneself as LGBT, first to oneself and later perhaps to others. Coming out usually occurs in several phases that range from personal acceptance of one's sexual orientation, disclosure of one's sexual orientation to others, and integrating one's sexual orientation into one's total personality (Evans and Broido, 1999; Stewart, 1995).

Theoretical Foundations Used with the LGBT Population

Numerous theoretical perspectives (Cass, 1979; Chapman and Brannock, 1987; Coleman, 1990; D'Augelli, 1994; Fassinger, 1998; Fassinger and Miller, 1997; McCarn and Fassinger, 1996; Sophie, 1985–1986; Troiden, 1989; Weinberg, Williams, and Pryor, 1994), ranging from general to specialized models, explore LGBT identity. Because space limitations do not permit detailed discussions of all these perspectives, this section provides a brief overview of the developmental theories of Fassinger and her colleagues; Cass; Weinberg, Williams, and Pryor; and Coleman. These theories represent examples of general and specialized models of LGBT identity development and are the theories most applicable to the detailed multimedia examples that follow.

Fassinger and Colleagues. Based on the work of McCarn and Fassinger (1996) on lesbian identity development, as well as the work of Fassinger and Miller (1997) on the applicability of McCarn and Fassinger's work to gay men, Fassinger's model examines growth in two components: personal identity and relationship identity (Fassinger, 1998). Fassinger and her colleagues propose that individuals simultaneously experience growth in both components as they develop a healthy gay, lesbian, or bisexual identity. They argue that identity development involves the establishment of an internal self-identity (personal identity) as well as the establishment of an identity within a minority group and how one changes in relation to other lesbians, gays, and bisexuals (relationship identity). They challenge the argument of previous models that identity disclosure is the ultimate sign of maturity and growth, and they state that these earlier models simply combine the search for individual and the search for group identification into a single process (Sanlo, 1998).

Cass. Cass (1979) presents her Sexual Identity Formation model as a representation of the coming-out process for gay men and lesbians. This six-stage model examines the internal transformations that individuals experience in accepting their homosexuality. Cass explains that as individuals experience increased tolerance of their homosexual identity by socializing with other homosexuals, they become able to integrate their personal homosexual identity into a fuller sense of identity.

Beginning with stage one, identity confusion, individuals become aware that they are not heterosexual and that being homosexual might describe their behavior and feelings. In this stage, individuals struggle with the question "Who am I?" and this usually results in one of three responses: initial acceptance that one is homosexual, elimination of all behaviors that reflect homosexuality, or denial that homosexuality is applicable.

Stage two, identity comparison, is characterized by an acceptance that being homosexual is a possibility. Individuals in this stage experience conflict and feelings of isolation and may even try to rationalize their feelings. Individuals experience numerous responses to this stage, ranging from internally recognizing their homosexual feelings but still publicly playing heterosexual to a total denial of their homosexuality.

Individuals in identity tolerance, stage three, understand that it is probable that they are homosexual. Greater contact with other homosexuals is sought. Movement through this stage depends on whether this contact is positive or negative. If the contact is negative, denial of homosexuality may continue. If the contact is positive, individuals will see the benefits of continued interaction with other homosexuals.

Identity acceptance, stage four, represents acceptance that one is homosexual. Increased personal comfort with being homosexual, continued contact with other gay men and lesbians, and selectivity in sharing one's homosexuality with others characterizes this stage. However, individuals in identity acceptance often continue to pass as heterosexual, which can lead to much conflict. Dealing with this conflict often drives individuals into stage five, identity pride.

Identity pride reflects a strong commitment to the gay and lesbian community. This pride, coupled with intense anger toward heterosexual privilege, exemplifies stage five. Pride is reflected in immersion in all things gay and lesbian.

Identity synthesis is the final stage of Cass's model. Individuals in this stage lessen their anger toward heterosexuals as they acknowledge similarities with heterosexuals and differences with other homosexuals. At this stage, an individual homosexual identity is integrated with the other components of one's identity.

Weinberg, Williams, and Pryor. The amount of research on bisexuality has been limited, and the results are often confusing. Bisexual identity development has often been included in earlier models of gay and lesbian identity development. In recent years, Fox (1995), Klein (1993), and Rust (1996) have proposed that this consolidation is inappropriate; they argue that identity development for bisexuals does not follow the same pattern as gay men and lesbians. Weinberg, Williams, and Pryor (1994) offer the most comprehensive bisexuality identity development model. The four stages of this model are initial confusion, finding and applying the label of bisexuality, settling into the identity, and continued uncertainty.

Coleman. Coleman (1981–1982, 1990) proposed a five-stage model of coming out. This model focuses on how gay and lesbian individuals develop and sustain interpersonal relationships. To successfully progress through this developmental model, individuals must successfully manage developmental tasks in order to achieve identity integration. This model applies to both males and females, and it postulates that individuals move both forward and backward in their progression, proceeding at varying rates. The five stages of the model are pre–coming out, coming out, exploration, first relationship, and integration.

A Brief History of LGBT Depictions in Television and Movies

LGBT individuals have had a varied depiction in the movies and television. The depiction of LGBT individuals has grown from nonexistent to very limited stereotypical roles to lead characters. Movies have included more LBGT characters than television has (Walters, 2001). Hadleigh (2001) reports that the earliest use of gay and lesbian characters in the movies was in the 1920s.

The early LGBT characters in movies were presented as peripheral or incidental characters and as stereotypes (Hadleigh, 2001); however, independent films presented LGBT characters as more complex (Walters, 2001). With an explosion of lesbian and gay film festivals since 1970 (Jones, 1999), LGBT characters are now presented as main characters in charge of their own lives (Walters, 2001), and mainstream films have made a shift since the 1990s to portraying lesbian and gay characters as respectable (Walters, 2001).

Early television avoided use of LGBT characters. The first discussions of homosexuality were in the 1950s, when locally produced talk shows and documentaries portrayed homosexuals as social and medical problems (Tropiano, 2002). During the 1950s and 1960s, homosexuality was seen as a social ill. In the 1970s, some television shows attempted to use their characters to educate viewers, but most characters remained stereotypical portrayals. Portrayals in the 1980s were a mixed bag; LGBT characters were central to some shows (*Northern Exposure* and *Thirtysomething*), but other shows (*Love Sydney*) trivialized gay and lesbian characters (Tropiano, 2002).

Since the 1990s, gay and lesbian characters have had an increased presence on television. In groundbreaking shows such *Ellen* and *Will and Grace* and in shows with positively portrayed gay and lesbian characters, such as *Dawson's Creek, Buffy the Vampire Slayer, Beverly Hills 90210*, and *Sex and the City*, gay characters are core cast members, coping with the same life stressors as heterosexual characters (Tropiano, 2002).

Portrayals of LGBT Individuals and the LGBT Community in Entertainment Media

As a student affairs graduate preparation program faculty member in a counselor education department, I regularly teach courses in student development theory and career counseling. To enhance student learning and application of the course concepts, I regularly use entertainment media (films, movies, and music). This section provides a list of resources that might be used in training and teaching others about the LGBT community, then presents two detailed examples. To facilitate use of these resources, they are organized into the following categories: gay men and lesbians, coming out, bisexual and transgender, homophobia, and discrimination.

A number of resources for teaching and training about LGBT issues are accessible. When choosing resources, select items that portray realistic perspectives on LGBT issues, not resources that encourage stereotypes and inaccuracies.

Gay Men and Lesbians. There are a number of excellent resources for educating others about the issues faced by gay men and lesbians. The two films *Go Fish* (1994) and *Desert Hearts* (1985) capture the essence of lesbian life and the development of lesbian identity. Other useful media resources include *Dykes to Watch Out For* (Bechdel, 1986), which chronicles the life of Mo, a lesbian cartoon character, and "Cicely" (1992), an episode of the television series *Northern Exposure*, which, when it aired, depicted one of only a few lesbian couples on television.

Love! Valour! Compassion! (1997) and *Long Time Companion* (1990) are two films that provide comprehensive representations of gay life and gay relationships. These resources also facilitate discussion of issues related to HIV/AIDS. Several books that chronicle the lives of gay characters can be effective teaching tools. These include *In Heat* (Mitchell, 1985), *28 Barbary Lane: A Tales of the City Omnibus* (Maupin, 1990), and *Back to Barbary Lane: The Final Tales of the City Omnibus* (Maupin, 1991).

A list of resources would be incomplete without mentioning the PBS show *P.O.V.* (1988-current). Since the late 1980s, this series has included the best in LGBT documentaries among its offerings. Episodes such as "Scout's Honor" (2001) (which focuses on twelve-year-old Steven Cozza and his attempts to change the Boy Scout ban on homosexuality) and "Golden Threads" (1999) (which focuses on the international association for older gay women that gives the episode its title) assist us in understanding of LGBT concerns.

Coming Out. I recommend the films *Trevor* (1994) and *Virgin Machine* (1988), and the books *Maurice* (Forster, 1987) and *A Boy's Own Story* (White, 2002) for educating others abut coming out. *Trevor,* only seventeen minutes long, showcases a thirteen-year-old who is dealing with being gay, and *Virgin Machine* chronicles the journey of a lesbian to self-acceptance.

Bisexual and Transgender. To help others learn about bisexual and transgender–related issues, the following media resources are suggested: The film *Boys Don't Cry* (1999) depicts the life of transsexual Brandon Teena. *Different for Girls* (1996), also a film, tells the story of the love that develops between a man and a post-operative transsexual. The song "Lola" (Davies, 1970) tells the story of a man who discovers that the woman he is attracted is a transsexual. "Boy, Girl, Boy, Girl" (2000), an episode of the television series *Sex and the City,* explores whether being bisexual is even possible.

Homophobia. It is my experience that locating resources depicting homophobia is more difficult than finding items in some of the other categories. Two episodes of the television series *Popular,* which portrays teen life in a California high school, examine homophobia. The episode called "Fag" (2001) deals with making derogatory jokes and the subsequent development of a gay and lesbian support group, while the episode "Booty Camp" (2000) focuses on the use of derogatory language. Easier to locate is a *Will and Grace* episode, "Will Works Out" (1999), that examines internalized homophobia.

An additional resource is Randy Shilts's *And the Band Played On* (Shilts, 2000). This book demonstrates how homophobia affected our country's response to the AIDS epidemic.

Discrimination. To increase students' understanding of the persecution that gay men have suffered, two films, *Bent* (1997) and *Paragraph 175* (2000) are suggested. *Bent* and *Paragraph 175* allow viewers to understand the treatment of gays during the Holocaust. Another useful resource that facilitates examination of workplace issues is *Out at Work* (1996). This film documents five years in the lives of two gay men and one lesbian as they struggle with job-related issues.

Teaching Students in a Graduate Preparation Program Class: *Defying Gravity*

This section presents a plot summary; goals, considerations, and process for use; and discussion questions.

Summary of Movie. A popular, straight-acting fraternity guy, Griff, is keeping secret his relationship with fraternity brother Pete. Pete is ready to accept his homosexuality, but Griff is not ready to accept that he is gay. A gay-bashing incident causes Griff to confront his sexuality, and he does so with the assistance of his friends Todd and Linna. *Defying Gravity* (1997) chronicles the evolution of Griff and Pete's relationship.

Goals of Activity. This movie can be used to accomplish the following goals: (1) to educate students about theories of homosexual identity development; (2) to examine the stereotyping and prejudices that gay men and lesbians experience; and (3) to provide students with opportunities to examine their personal beliefs and values.

Considerations. In using this movie, attention should be paid to the size of the class, the time required for the activity, materials needed, and classroom setup. Class size is only an issue if you need to divide the larger class into smaller process groups. For processing of the film, use small groups of no more than five individuals, so that all participants can participate equally in the discussion. The few materials needed for this activity include a DVD of the movie, markers and paper, and a list of discussion and process questions. To facilitate involvement, a room with movable chairs is preferred.

Process. To provide an optimal learning environment, the instructor and the class must be prepared. The instructor should watch the movie prior to using it in class. I use this particular movie because students relate well to it. Two options can be used in showing the movie. As this film is only ninety-three minutes long and I teach in a graduate program with three-hour class periods, I typically show the entire movie uninterrupted, then follow it with discussion. However, if class time is limited, you can show preselected scenes that illustrate key points. One modification of this process is to assign viewing of the film outside of class. You may wish to place a copy on reserve in the library or media center.

To prepare students for the film, related readings can be distributed one week prior to the movie's screening. These readings should focus on LGBT issues, specifically on lesbian and gay identity development models.

In the first thirty minutes of the class period in which you show the movie, discuss LGBT issues and identity development. After this brief overview, provide the class with the process questions that you are using to frame the class discussion. This allows students to watch the movie from an educational perspective, not simply as entertainment. Show the movie, challenging students to watch for answers to the discussion questions. After the movie, a short break may be taken, if you wish. To conclude the activity, the small groups are instructed to discuss the film, using the discussion questions. Plan to spend forty-five minutes to an hour processing in small groups and as a larger class.

Discussion Questions. What stereotypes and prejudices occur in the movie?

What theoretical perspectives of homosexual identity development could be applied to the characters of Griff, Pete, and Linna?

How realistic is this movie in its portrayal of gay men and lesbians? Explain. What would you do to assist Griff, Pete, and Linna?

How does this movie make you feel and think about gay men and lesbians? What are your personal reactions?

What types of campus resources could be used to assist these characters?

Teaching Student Staff About LGBT: "I'm Coming Out"

A content summary; goals, considerations, and process for use; and discussion questions receive attention.

Summary of Television Episode. "I'm Coming Out" (2002), an episode from the television series *True Life,* chronicles the coming-out stories of four characters—Joel, Dora, Matt, and Jayce—as they reveal their sexual orientation identity to family and friends. Each story is very personal and moving.

Goals of Activity. The goals of this activity are (1) to educate students about the coming-out process; and (2) to allow students an opportunity to hear personal stories of coming out.

Considerations. This forty-five-minute video can be used as a training tool with any type of student group. Individuals seeking to purchase copies of this video should begin by calling the MTV Educational Request Hotline to get information on placing a video order and the charge for the video. All orders must be made in writing (no phone or Web orders are accepted), explaining how the video will be used and acknowledging familiarity with the subject matter, and sent to Music Television's Rights and Clearance Department in New York City.

Because of the emotions generated in those who watch this video, it works best with groups no larger than thirty individuals. If the group is larger, add facilitators. To use this video in a training workshop, no materials other than the video are necessary. I suggest presenting the video in a workshop of approximately two hours, in an area that provides comfortable seating, ideally in a circle. One benefit of this video is that you can show only part of it and not lose any effectiveness.

Process. Prior to showing the video, describe Coleman's stages of coming out. Explain to the participants that this video is about four individuals, who share their coming-out stories. Encourage participants to listen closely to the stories and monitor their personal reactions and feelings. Once the video is completed, allow participants a few minutes to internally process their reactions. In small groups, take approximately twenty minutes to talk about the discussion questions. After completion of that assignment, ask each group to report their responses to the larger group. As the trainer, you can develop your own questions or use the lesson plan provided on the MTV Web site.

Discussion Questions. What were your reactions to each individual's coming-out story?
What patterns did you observe as these stories were told?
Which stage of Coleman's coming-out model was each of the four characters experiencing?
As a student leader, what would you do to assist each individual in their coming-out process?

Conclusion

Discussing LGBT issues is sometimes difficult for both students and student affairs practitioners. Using movies, television shows, popular music, and books can focus discussion and illustrate key principles and ideas. A number of resources are available to assist in educating students on LGBT issues. These resources can facilitate understanding of LGBT identity development, foster insight into and exploration of LGBT psychological and sociological issues, and provide strategies for assisting LGBT students in understanding their sexuality.

References

Barret B., and Logan, C. *Counseling Gay Men and Lesbians*. Pacific Grove, Calif.: Brooks/Cole, 2002.

Bechdel, A. *Dykes to Watch Out For*. Ithaca, N.Y.: Firebrand Books, 1986.

Bent [motion picture]. United Kingdom and Japan: MGM Home Entertainment, 1997.

"Booty Camp" [television series episode]. *Popular*. United States: Warner Brothers, 2000.

"Boy, Girl, Boy, Girl" [television series episode]. *Sex and the City*. United States: Home Box Office, 2000.

Boys Don't Cry [motion picture]. United States: Fox Searchlight, 1999.

Cass, V. C. "Homosexual Identity Formation: A Theoretical Model." *Journal of Homosexuality*, 1979, 4(3), 219–235.

Chapman, B. E., and Brannock, J. C. "Proposed Model of Lesbian Identity Development: An Empirical Examination." *Journal of Homosexuality*, 1987, 14(3–4), 69–80.

"Cicely" [television series episode]. *Northern Exposure*. United States: Columbia Broadcasting System, 1992.

Coleman, E. "Developmental Stages of the Coming Out Process." *Journal of Homosexuality*, 1981–1982, 7(2–3), 31–43.

Coleman, E. "Toward a Synthetic Understanding of Sexual Orientation." In D. P. McWhirter, S. A. Sanders, and J. M. Reinisch (eds.), *Homosexuality/Heterosexuality: Concepts of Sexual Orientation*. New York: Oxford University Press, 1990.

D'Augelli, A. R. "Identity Development and Sexual Orientation: Toward a Model of Lesbian, Gay, and Bisexual Development." In E. J. Trickett, R. J. Watts, and D. Birman (eds.), *Human Diversity: Perspectives on People in Context*. San Francisco: Jossey-Bass, 1994.

Davies, R. D. "Lola." [Recorded by The Kinks]. Record album, *Come Dancing with the Kinks*. United States: BMI, 1970.

Defying Gravity [motion picture]. United States: Boom Pictures, 1997.

Desert Hearts [motion picture]. United States and Canada: Metro-Goldwyn-Mayer, 1985.

Different for Girls [motion picture]. United Kingdom and France: British Broadcasting Corporation, 1996.

Evans, N. J., and Broido, E. M. "Coming Out in College Residence Halls: Negotiation, Meaning Making, Challenges, Supports." *Journal of College Student Development*, 1999, 40(6), 658–668.

"Fag" [television series episode]. *Popular*. United States: Warner Brothers, 2001.

Fassinger, R. E. "Lesbian, Gay, and Bisexual Identity and Student Development Theory." In R. L. Sanlo (ed.), *Working with Lesbian, Gay, Bisexual, and Transgender College Students: A Handbook for Faculty and Administrators*. Westport, CT: Greenwood Press, 1998.

Fassinger, R. E., and Miller, B. A. "Validation of an Inclusive Model of Sexual Minority Identity Formation on a Sample of Gay Men." *Journal of Homosexuality*, 1997, 32(2), 53–78.

Forster, E. M. *Maurice*. New York: Norton, 1987.

Fox, R. C. "Bisexual Identities." In A. R. D'Augelli and C. J. Patterson (eds.), *Lesbian, Gay, and Bisexual Identities over the Lifespan: Psychological Perspectives*. New York: Oxford University Press, 1995.

Go Fish [motion picture]. United States: Metro-Goldwyn-Mayer, 1994.

"Golden Threads" [television series episode]. *P.O.V.* United States: Public Broadcasting System, 1999.

Hadleigh, B. *The Lavender Screen*. New York: Kensington, 2001.

"I'm Coming Out" [television series episode]. *True Life*. United States: Music Television Network, 2002.

Jones, C. "Lesbian and Gay Cinema." In J. Nelmes (ed.), *An Introduction to Film Studies*. New York: Routledge, 1999.

Klein, F. *The Bisexual Option.* New York: Harrington Park Press, 1993.

Long Time Companion [motion picture]. United States: Metro-Goldwyn-Mayer, 1990.

Love! Valour! Compassion! [motion picture]. United States: Fine Line Features, 1997.

Maupin, A. *28 Barbary Lane: A Tales of the City Omnibus.* New York: HarperCollins, 1990.

Maupin, A. *Back to Barbary Lane: The Final Tales of the City Omnibus.* New York: HarperCollins, 1991.

McCarn, S. R., and Fassinger, R. E. "Revisioning Sexual Minority Identity Formation: A New Model for Lesbian Identity and Its Implications for Counseling and Research." *The Counseling Psychologist,* 1996, *24*(3), 508–534.

Mitchell, L. *In Heat.* New York: Gay Presses of New York, 1985.

Morrow, G. D. "Bisexuality: An Exploratory Review." *Annals of Sex Research,* 1989, *2,* 283–306.

Out at Work [motion picture]. United States: Andersongold Films, 1996.

Paragraph 175 [motion picture]. United States: New Yorker Films, 2000.

Rust, P. C. "Monogamy and Polyamory: Relationship Issues for Bisexuals." In B. A. Firestein (ed.), *Bisexuality: The Psychology and Politics of an Invisible Minority.* Thousand Oaks, CA: Sage, 1996.

Ryan, C., and Futterman, D. *Lesbian and Gay Youth.* New York: Columbia University Press, 1998.

Sanlo, R. *Working with Lesbian, Gay, Bisexual and Transgender College Students.* Westport, CT: Greenwood Press, 1998.

"Scout's Honor" [television series episode]. *P.O.V.* United States: Public Broadcasting System, 2001.

Shilts, R. *And the Band Played On.* New York: St. Martin's Press, 2000.

Sophie, J. "A Critical Examination of Stage Theories of Lesbian Identity Development." *Journal of Homosexuality, 12*(2–3), 1985–1986, 39–51.

Stewart, W. *Cassell's Queer Companion.* New York: Cassell Wellington House, 1995.

Trevor [motion picture]. United States: Water Bearer Films, 1994.

Troiden, R. R. "The Formation of Homosexual Identities." *Journal of Homosexuality,* 1989, *17*(1–2), 43–73.

Tropiano, S. *Prime Time Closet: A History of Gays and Lesbians on TV.* New York: Applause Theatre Cinema, 2002.

Virgin Machine [motion picture]. West Germany: Hyane Films, 1988.

Walters, S. D. *All the Rage.* Chicago: University of Chicago Press, 2001.

Weinberg, M. S., Williams, C. J., and Pryor, D. W. *Dual Attractions: Understanding Bisexuality.* New York: Oxford University Press, 1994.

White, E. *A Boy's Own Story.* Westminister, Md.: Modern Library, 2002.

"Will Works Out" [television series episode]. *Will and Grace.* United States: National Broadcasting Corporation, 1999.

TONY W. CAWTHON is associate professor of student affairs and unit coordinator in counselor education at Clemson University in Clemson, South Carolina.

5

This chapter presents several strategies for teaching about sex and gender using entertainment media and explores critical issues related to content development, the delivery process, and evaluation methods.

Using Entertainment Media to Inform Student Affairs Teaching and Practice Related to Sex and Gender

Tracy L. Davis

"You play ball like a girl" (*The Sandlot,* 1993). This phrase, shouted in a singsong manner, is the final insult in a litany of put-downs exchanged between competing boys' baseball teams in the movie *The Sandlot.* Viewers generally laugh at this scene. Many continue watching the movie while remaining unreflective about the gendered messages being conveyed. After all, one film comment is not necessarily indicative of sexism in the media. Kilbourne (2000), in *Killing Us Softly III,* argues that the single sound bite, however, is not as problematic as the powerful cumulative effect these messages have over time. Similarly, according to Kellner (1995), persistent gendered messages shape "our view of the world and deepest values. . . . [and] define what is considered good or bad, positive or negative, moral or evil" (p. 1).

In American culture, media impact is pervasive. The average American household, for example, has the television on for seven hours each day (Holtzman, 2000). In addition, adolescents see 20,000 television advertisements each year (Smith, 1994), watch hours of music videos each week (Signorielli, McLeod, and Healy, 1994), and increasingly play video games (Gardyn, 2003). It is estimated that "current students will see more of television than the classroom by the time they graduate, and by their mid-20s they will be watching television as the third major time-consuming activity of any given day, after work and sleep" (Davis, 1990, p. 325).

NEW DIRECTIONS FOR STUDENT SERVICES, no. 108, Winter 2004 © Wiley Periodicals, Inc.

Statistics about the ubiquitousness of media are alarming in light of significant research uncovering gender bias. Studies have found traditional sex-role scripting and sex bias in several forms of media, including films (Eschholz, Bufkin, and Long, 2002; Kissling, 2002; Oliver, Sargent, and Weaver, 1998); magazines (Carpenter, 1998; Kolbe and Albanese, 1997; Thomas and Treiber, 2000); television programs (Lauzen and Dozier, 2002; Klumas and Marchant, 1994); video games (Deitz, 1998); advertisements (Blaine and McElroy, 2002; Pierce and McBride, 1999; Stephenson, Stover, and Villamor, 1997); and comics (Brabant and Mooney, 1997). Moreover, several studies link television viewing with adherence to sexist views and traditional gender roles (Signorielli, 1989; Suls and Gastoff, 1981; Tedesco, 1974) as well as a correlation between men's adherence to traditional roles and sexual assault (Bernard, Bernard, and Bernard, 1985; Pagelow, 1981).

This chapter will explore the use of popular books, advertisements, television, and film as methods for interrupting the potential negative impact that media messages have on healthy sex-role development. First, a conceptual basis for using media to promote learning about gender and sex is briefly discussed. The conceptual concerns identified should be considered both before and during curriculum development. Next, I present a broad discussion related to program content and process issues associated with using popular fiction, television commercials, situation comedies and dramas, films, and documentaries to promote student learning about gender and sex. I conclude with some questions about the effectiveness of using entertainment media to promote learning about gender and sex roles.

Conceptual Foundation

The conceptual basis for using media to promote learning about sex roles is grounded in Bandura's social learning theory (Bandura, 1977). According to social learning theory, a multitude of cultural influences affect sex-role development, and media such as film and television are important vehicles for socialization. Cultural traditions and beliefs about appropriate sex roles are transmitted through imitation and modeling. Thus, sex-role messages found in television and other media are seen as powerful cultural influences.

Using entertainment media to deconstruct powerful sex-role messages is an ideal method for promoting learning about gender identity development. The deconstruction process is based on a constructivist teaching philosophy. Drawing primarily on Piaget (1954) and Vygotsky (1978), constructivism emphasizes the notion that individuals are constructors of their own knowledge rather than simply reproducers of set laws or facts. Human beings, thus, construct knowledge as they attempt to bring meaning to their experience through assimilation and accommodation (Piaget, 1954). Teachers and students bring what they have previously learned about appropriate sex roles and are challenged to consider both the sources through which sex roles have been learned as well as the messages that have shaped their values. The classroom becomes a social milieu in which the complex interaction between individual and society is reproduced and exploited in order to promote explorations of alternative views.

By treating media portrayals of gender as consequential, educators can use video clips and fiction to explore gaps between socially prescribed messages and individually chosen values. Students are challenged to more clearly understand how they have built bridges over these chasms in the past and how they might choose to construct a different connection. For example, an instructor might ask, "What impact does a certain portrayal of the protagonist have on men and women, as well as boys and girls, who are watching a prime-time television show?" Dervin (1989) suggests that the impact will vary from person to person through an active process of sense making. Moreover, the didactic strategy implicit in sense making is questioning or interviewing. General questions might include the following: What ideas about gender and sex are being promoted? How useful have you found these images in becoming who you are? What limits do you feel are imposed by these ideas? What barriers stand between you and deciding to reconstruct an image more consistent with who you are? Dervin (1989) states "an important aspect of sense-making methods is that they are all situated in real moments in time-space. . . . and posit no hypothetical questions to respondents, nor do they present elaborate lists of options as defined by institutions to which respondents must reply" (p. 79). The sense-making interview strategy, thus, avoids selling orthodoxy by allowing learners to reach their own conclusions.

Program Process Strategies

While program content areas need to be thoughtfully constructed and guided by theory, the success of any didactic intervention often depends on the processes through which the program is implemented. Program processes are aimed at making the content palatable to the learner, effectively engaging the learner, reducing defensiveness, and facilitating critical evaluation of the information being presented. That is, process strategies should be geared toward enhancing the "learnability" of intended outcomes. Since developmental interventions using constructivist pedagogy require providing divergent viewpoints about sex and gender that raise participant defenses, it is important that program developers meet this challenge directly and use facilitative styles and strategies that promote learning. Strategies include focusing on personal experience, deconstructing media messages, reconstructing knowledge in a nondogmatic fashion, and creating a safe learning environment.

Focus on Personal Experience. In any course or workshop I teach on a multicultural issue, I encourage reflection about personal experiences and history. Examining personal experiences allows us to determine what we have learned informally about men and women and how we came to these beliefs. For example, in my student development theory course, which focuses on identities, the first assignment requires students to reflect on their family background, racial and cultural heritage, religious beliefs, sexual orientation, gender, and socioeconomic status. A variety of questions can be offered to raise awareness about how personal experience with each of these identities shapes us. An important aspect of encouraging students to reflect on their own experience is that it promotes "I" statements and makes culture influence explicit.

Since sharing personal history can be threatening, I sometimes share a personal anecdote about my own gender identity development. I believe this models appropriate disclosure as well as creates a less judgmental learning environment. That is, by admitting my humanness and developmental past, I try to communicate that we are all products of social influence and that we now have an opportunity to consider whether culturally transmitted messages about gender fit with our personal experience.

Deconstruction of Media Messages and Nondogmatic Reconstruction of Knowledge. Using videos and other media both effectively engages participants and reduces defensiveness, thus preparing students to learn. A key to deconstructing passively received messages about gender is to encourage active or critical viewing. Critical viewing is accomplished by asking careful follow-up questions aimed at challenging learners to think critically about underlying sex-role messages. Virtually any video clip that illustrates sex-role differences is appropriate. Essentially, participants are challenged to become critical consumers of the messages they receive.

After evaluating media messages, participants are encouraged to develop their own beliefs about sex roles. This process offers participants the opportunity to reconsider the messages that they previously absorbed uncritically and then independently reconstruct their own knowledge. The teacher assumes the role of facilitator, not lecturer or expert. Participants are not pressured to change their beliefs; rather, they are invited to analyze new information and assimilate this knowledge, integrating it with what they have previously learned. Another advantage of using video to reconstruct knowledge is that it provides supervised practice in becoming a critical consumer of potentially dysfunctional messages.

Creation of a Safe Learning Environment. Since discussing messages about gender and sex can be controversial, the environment should be psychologically safe and conducive to meaningful sharing of personal beliefs. Depending on how well the participants know one another, I generally ask what ground rules for discussion they would like to establish. I typically state, for example, that we should speak from our experience and seek first to understand, then to be understood. In addition, I have sometimes offered the following "safe environment contract": "I understand that it's OK to be imperfect with regard to communicating about sex and gender. It's OK if I don't know all of the answers. I have permission to ask questions that may appear stupid. I am a product of a culture that makes it difficult to discuss issues of sex and gender; I don't have to feel guilty about what I know or believe, but I do need to take responsibility for what I can do now."

Another aspect of creating a safe learning context is attending to the developmental needs of the group. Carney, Taylor, and Stevens (1986) offer a model for facilitating sex-role transitions that recommends a highly structured learning environment with facilitators who offer more support than challenge for learners who are new to discussions of sex and gender. For more sophisticated groups, more challenge and less structure can be offered. Similarly, Kegan (1982) offers a framework for creating supportive conditions in which students can open up to and engage new ideas, grapple with contradictions, and then incorporate new ways of making sense. Students first defend their positions and then surrender to inconsistencies before finally reintegrating new knowledge. Kegan outlines learning strategies that are appropriate at each stage.

Program Content

While presentation process issues affect the effectiveness of program delivery, program content should be meaningfully constructed on the scaffolding of developmental theory. Models and theories related to gender identity development include Belenky, Clinchy, Goldberger and Tarule's (1986) discussion of women's ways of knowing, Josselson's (1987, 1996) research into women's identity development, O'Neil's (1990) theory of male gender role conflict, Pollack's (1999) and Davis's (2002) interviews of young men, Jones and McEwen's (2000) multiple dimensions of identity model, and, of course, Gilligan's (1982) landmark work on women's and men's moral orientation. In the discussion of program content, I will give examples of how I use popular fiction, television programs and commercials, film, and documentaries to promote learning about sex and gender. The focus will be on what student affairs professionals can do to promote healthy sex-role development in college men and women, using entertainment media. Key intervention objectives include helping participants explore their own attitudes and listen to others' opinions about sex roles; understand how media contributes to sex-role development; deconstruct potentially harmful sex-role socialization messages embedded in the popular media; and identify healthy alternative models.

Popular Books. An assignment I use in my developmental theory course requires students to read a piece of popular fiction or nonfiction. Two examples of gender-related books they can choose are *Becoming a Man* (Monette, 1992) and *Like Water for Chocolate* (Esquivel, 1992). Students are asked to write a paper that focuses on the sex roles communicated in the text, the identity development of the protagonists, and contexts in which developmental changes take place.

Students are asked to apply developmental theory on gender and sex to characters in the book. For example, in Esquivel's *Like Water for Chocolate*

(Esquivel, 1992), the protagonist, Tita, is a complex character, and the story is rich with material related to gender identity development. Students can use Jones and McEwen's model of multiple dimensions of identity to discuss the intersections between Tita's gender and Mexican heritage (Jones and McEwen, 2000). They can explore how these identities interact with the historical period, family traditions, and the broader culture to construct limits. Students can also illustrate how Tita shakes off the bonds of tradition to move from received knowledge to constructed knowledge as represented in Belenky, Clinchy, Goldberger, and Tarule's (1986) model of women's ways of knowing.

Popular books offer characters whose developmental changes can be explored in order to learn about the construction of sex-role attitudes and behaviors. Cultural contexts can also be compared across stories to explore how unique circumstances (for example, historical period, religion, family, serendipity, and so on) coalesce to stimulate or inhibit growth. On the day that students submit this assignment, we have a discussion that explores how social circumstances affect development, compares protagonists from similar cultures, and suggests interventions that might shift the story line.

Television Commercials. Blaine and McElroy (2002) report that product advertisements constitute approximately fifteen minutes of each hour of programming and are not a trivial component of the television landscape. While the literature clearly documents sex-role stereotypes in television advertising (for example, Courtney and Whipple, 1980; Hall and Crum, 1994) and their effects on viewers' attitudes (Beckwith, 1994; Lavine, Sweeney, and Wagner, 1999), students often think I am making too big an issue out of the humorous anecdotes offered in commercials. To demonstrate the impact that commercials might have, students are asked to view about an hour of children's television and watch only the commercials. After viewing several advertisements, they are asked to consider what gender-related messages are being communicated, what language is used, whether boys and girls are directed toward different activities and toys, whether there are gender differences in the voice-over, and so on.

Students are often shocked at the differences in voice tone and language used in the commercials aimed at girls compared with those aimed at boys. Interestingly, many women in the class often claim that they played with or would want to use the products offered in the "boys' commercials," but few (if any) male students offer similar sentiments about the "girls' commercials." Students are also surprised at the absence of the opposite sex in many of the commercials and at stereotypes that are reinforced. In one Barbie® advertisement, for example, the girls playing with the dolls are cooking dinner and inquiring, "Where's Ken?" when it is time to eat.

A variation on using television commercials is bringing copies of popular magazines and asking students to clip advertisements representing gender themes. As in the critique of commercials, I ask students to comment on who is pictured, what language and slogan are used, and what sex-role stereotypes are being represented.

Television Sitcoms and Dramas. Research into gender roles portrayed on prime-time network television has shown that men and women are often portrayed in stereotypical ways (Browne, 1998; Glascock, 2001; Greenberg and Collette, 1997; Signorielli, 1989). Television sitcoms and dramas are rich with material that can be used for learning about gender and sexuality. Student affairs professionals can examine how programs represent the roles of men and women—for example, by observing which occupations are depicted, how nurturing or aggressive behaviors are portrayed, or even, taking a historical perspective, how gender roles have changed over the years.

One of the most popular sitcoms of this decade is *Friends* (2003). This half-hour show is fertile ground for illustrations of relationships and sex roles. In addition to its popularity, an advantage of this program is that about half of the episodes are currently available on DVDs. Clips can be used, for example, to connect behavior to one of the four factors in O'Neil's theory of gender-role conflict or to illustrate important men's developmental issues (such as fear of femininity) (O'Neil, 1990) that result in male behaviors such as side-by-side communication and other forms of male expression. Side-by-side communication, for example, refers to research that suggests men are more comfortable sharing with other men when sitting next to one another rather than face to face (Davis, 2002; Pollack, 1999).

I have also used the six main characters on *Friends* (Ross, Rachel, Joey, Monica, Phoebe, and Chandler) to illustrate the Carney, Taylor, and Stevens (1986) model of sex-role transitions. After discussing the stages of the model, I first ask participants to name the six characters. Students are immediately able to list the characters' names; this fact alone illustrates the significant impact that television has on our consciousness. I then ask participants to match each of the six characters with a stage in the sex-role transitions model and give a rationale based on the character's behavior. For example, many place Joey at the pre-awareness stage, based on both his simple-minded misunderstandings and his seemingly unreflective adherence to traditional gender roles.

In addition to sitcoms, television dramas often present issues related to gender and sex. Although clips related to gender and sex are common in many programs, I have found *Boston Public, The Real World,* and *The West Wing* to be particularly fruitful. Students are challenged to view programs through the lens of gender. Questions can be raised, for example, about which of Josselson's identity status categories—foreclosed, moratorium, achieved, or diffuse—might best describe various female characters (Josselson, 1996). In addition, students can be asked to consider whether the moral voice of each character reflects a care orientation or a justice orientation (Gilligan, 1982). The definition of feminism and issues related to sexual harassment can also be introduced into the discussion.

Assessing the Effectiveness of Using Media

There is some evidence that using entertainment media to promote learning about gender issues is effective. Nathanson, Wilson, McGee, and Sebastian (2002), for example, used active mediation to successfully reduce the harmful effects of gender-stereotyped television. The researchers contradicted information contained in television programs by refuting the accuracy of stereotyped depictions to elementary school children. Johnson and Ettema (1982) also found that children's exposure to nontraditional gender roles in television programs was related to holding fewer gender stereotypes, especially when the content was discussed as part of the curriculum. Although these results might suggest that using a critical media approach to promote learning about sex and gender issues is highly effective, such a claim remains elusive. Few interventions have been systematically evaluated. One glaring hole in the literature is research that addresses whether using entertainment media to promote learning in college programs or graduate school classrooms is effective.

While empirical investigations are needed, I have collected some evidence that using media to promote learning about sex and gender may be successful. Students have rated favorably the courses in which I use a significant amount of video programming. Comments from students and program participants include the following: "[The videos are] engaging and make me think about applying what I have learned to actual situations." "The commercials were shocking. . . . I'll be more conscious about how I watch them."

Summary

We student development educators can successfully use various forms of entertainment media to promote learning about gender and sex if we carefully construct educational programs with a sound theoretical foundation. Social learning theory and constructivist teaching methods offer the best frameworks for understanding media's impact and developing appropriate interventions. Using theory to shape the content of our interventions is, however, insufficient for developing an effective program aimed at raising awareness about gender development and sex roles. Critical process and delivery issues need to be thoughtfully implemented in order to promote engagement, create an environment conducive to learning, and encourage student reconstruction of their knowledge. Finally, to ensure that the use of entertainment media is purposeful and effective, student affairs professionals need to identify specific objectives as well as strategies to assess whether those objectives are met.

References

Bandura, A. *Social Learning Theory*. Englewood Cliffs, N.J.: Prentice Hall, 1977.

Beckwith, J. "Terminology and Social Relevance in Psychological Research on Gender." *Social Behavior and Personality*, 1994, 22(4), 329–336.

Belenky, M. F., Clinchy, B. M., Goldberger, N. R., and Tarule, J. M. *Women's Ways of Knowing: The Development of Self, Voice and Mind*. New York: Basic Books, 1986.

Bernard, J. L., Bernard, S., and Bernard, M. L. "Courtship Violence and Sex-Typing." *Family Relations*, 1985, 34(4), 573–576.

Blaine, B., and McElroy, J. "Selling Stereotypes: Weight Loss Infomercials, Sexism, and Weightism." *Sex Roles*, 2002, 46(9–10), 351–357.

Brabant, S., and Mooney, L. A. "Sex Role Stereotyping in the Sunday Comics: A Twenty-Year Update." *Sex Roles*, 1997, 37(8), 269–281.

Browne, B. A. "Gender Stereotypes in Advertising on Children's Television in the 1990s: A Cross-National Analysis." *Journal of Advertising*, 1998, 27(1), 83–96.

Carney, C., Taylor, K., and Stevens, M. "Sex Roles in Groups: A Developmental Approach." *Journal for Specialists in Group Work*, 1986, 11(4), 200–208.

Carpenter, L. M. "From Girls into Women: Scripts for Sexuality and Romance in *Seventeen* Magazine, 1974–1994." *Journal of Sex Research*, 1998, 35(2), 158–168.

Courtney, A., and Whipple, T. *Sex Stereotyping in Advertising*. Lexington, Mass.: Lexington Books, 1980.

Davis, D. M. "Portrayals of Women in Prime-Time Network Television: Some Demographic Characteristics." *Sex Roles*, 1990, 23(5–6), 325–332.

Davis, T. L. "Voices of Gender Role Conflict: The Social Construction of College Men's Identity." *Journal of College Student Development*, 2002, 43(4), 508–521.

Deitz, T. "An Examination of Violence and Gender Role Portrayals in Video Games: Implications for Gender Socialization and Aggressive Behavior." *Sex Roles*, 1998, 38(5–6), 425–442.

Dervin, B. "Audience as Listener and Learner, Teacher and Confidante: The Sense-Making Approach." In R. E. Rice and C. K. Atkin (eds.), *Public Communication Campaigns*. (2nd ed.) Thousand Oaks, Calif.: Sage, 1989.

Eschholz, S., Bufkin, J., and Long, J. "Symbolic Reality Bites: Women and Racial/Ethnic Minorities in Modern Film." *Sociological Spectrum*, 2002, 22(3), 299–334.

Esquivel, L. *Like Water for Chocolate*. New York: Doubleday, 1992.

Friends [television series]. United States: Warner Home Video, 2003.

Gardyn, R. "Got Game?" *American Demographics*, 2003, 25(8), 18.

Gilligan, C. *In a Different Voice*. Cambridge, Mass.: Harvard University Press, 1982.

Glascock, J. "Gender Roles on Prime-Time Network Television: Demographics and Behaviors." *Journal of Broadcasting and Electronic Media*, 2001, 45(4), 656–669.

Greenberg, B. S., and Collette, L. "The Changing Faces of TV: A Demographic Analysis of Network Television's New Seasons, 1966–1992." *Journal of Broadcasting and Electronic Media*, 1997, 41(1), 1–13.

Hall, C., and Crum, M. "Women and Body-isms in Television Beer Commercials." *Sex Roles*, 1994, 31(5–6), 329–337.

Holtzman, L. *Media Messages: What Film, Television, and Popular Music Teach Us About Race, Class, Gender and Sexual Orientation*. Armonk, N.Y.: Sharpe, 2000.

Johnson, J., and Ettema, J. S. *Positive Images: Breaking Stereotypes with Children's Television*. Thousand Oaks, Calif.: Sage, 1982.

Jones, S. R., and McEwen, M. K. "A Conceptual Model of Multiple Dimensions of Identity." *Journal of College Student Development*, 2000, 41(4), 405–414.

Josselson, R. *Finding Herself: Pathways to Identity Development in Women*. San Francisco: Jossey-Bass, 1987.

Josselson, R. *Revising Herself: The Story of Women's Identity from College to Midlife*. New York: Oxford University Press, 1996.

Kegan, R. *The Evolving Self*. Cambridge, Mass.: Harvard University Press, 1982.

Kellner, D. *Media Culture: Cultural Studies, Identity and Politics Between the Modern and the Postmodern*. London: Routledge, 1995.

Kilbourne, J. *Killing Us Softly III: Advertising's Image of Women*. Northhampton, Mass.: Media Education Foundation, 2000. Videotape.

Kissling, E. A. "On the Rag on Screen: Menarche in Film and Television." *Sex Roles*, 2002, 46(1–2), 5–12.

Klumas, A. L., and Marchant, T. "Images of Men in Popular Sitcoms." *Journal of Men's Studies*, 1994, 2(3), 269–285.

Kolbe, R. H., and Albanese, P. J. "The Functional Integration of Sole-Male Images into Magazine Advertisements." *Sex Roles*, 1997, 36(11–12), 813–836.

Lauzen, M. M., and Dozier, D. M. "You Look Mahvelous: An Examination of Gender and Appearance Comments in the 1999–2000 Prime-Time Season." *Sex Roles*, 2002, 46(11–12), 429–437.

Lavine, H., Sweeney, D. and Wagner, S. "Depicting Women as Sex Objects in Television Advertising: Effects on Body Dissatisfaction." *Personality and Social Psychology Bulletin*, 1999, 25(8), 1049–1058.

Monette, P. *Becoming a Man: Half a Life Story*. Orlando, Fla.: Harcourt Brace Jovanovich, 1992.

Nathanson, A., Wilson, B., McGee, J., and Sebastian, M. "Counteracting the Effects of Female Stereotypes on Television via Active Mediation." *Journal of Communication*, 2002, 52(4), 922–937.

Oliver, M. B., Sargent, S. L., and Weaver, J. B. "The Impact of Sex and Gender Role Self-Perception on Affective Reactions to Different Types of Film." *Sex Roles*, 1998, 38(1–2), 45–62.

O'Neil, J. M. "Assessing Men's Gender Role Conflict." In D. Moore and F. Leafgren (eds.), *Problem Solving Strategies and Interventions for Men in Conflict*. Alexandria, Va.: American Counseling Association, 1990.

Pagelow, M. D. *Women Battering Victims and Their Experiences*. Thousand Oaks, Calif.: Sage, 1981.

Piaget, J. *The Construction of Reality in the Child*. (M. Cook, trans.). New York: Basic Books, 1954.

Pierce, K., and McBride, M. "Aunt Jemima Isn't Keeping Up with the Energizer Bunny: Stereotyping of Animated Spokes Characters in Advertising." *Sex Roles*, 1999, 40(11–12), 959–968.

Pollack, W. S. *Real Boys: Rescuing Our Sons from the Myths of Boyhood*. New York: Henry Holt, 1999.

The Sandlot [motion picture]. United States: Twentieth-Century Fox, 1993.

Signorielli, N. "Television and Conceptions About Sex Roles: Maintaining Conventionality and the Status Quo." *Sex Roles*, 1989, 21(5–6), 341–360.

Signorielli, N., McLeod, D., and Healy, E. "Gender Stereotypes in MTV Commercials: The Beat Goes On." *Journal of Broadcasting and Electronic Media*, 1994, 38(1), 91–101.

Smith, L. J. "A Content Analysis of Gender Differences in Children's Advertising." *Journal of Broadcasting and Electronic Media*, 1994, 38(3), 323–337.

Stephenson, T., Stover, W. J., and Villamor, M. "Sell Me Some Prestige! The Portrayal of Women in Business-Related Ads." *Journal of Popular Culture*, 1997, 30(Spring), 255–271.

Suls, J., and Gastoff, J. "The Incidence of Sex Discrimination, Sexual Content, and Hostility in TV Humor." *Journal of Applied Communication Research*, 1981, 9(1), 42–49.

Tedesco, N. "Patterns in Prime Time." *Journal of Communications,* 1974, *24*(2), 119–124.

Thomas, M. E., and Treiber, L. A. "Race, Gender, and Status: A Content Analysis of Print Advertisements in Four Popular Magazines." *Sociological Spectrum,* 2000, *20*(3), 357–371.

Vygotsky, L. S. *Mind in Society: The Development of Higher Psychological Processes.* (M. Cook, trans.). Cambridge, Mass.: Harvard University Press, 1978.

TRACY L. DAVIS is associate professor of college student personnel in the Department of Educational and Interdisciplinary Studies at Western Illinois University in Macomb, Illinois.

6

This chapter provides a simple and effective model for using film, television and other popular media in student leadership development activities.

Using Entertainment Media to Inform Student Affairs Teaching and Practice Related to Leadership

Timothy R. McMahon, Ron Bramhall

One of the purposes of higher education is to develop students into leaders (Astin and Astin, 1995). While the development of student leaders happens throughout the academy, much of it is done by student affairs staff members through teaching, training, advising, and mentoring. Using entertainment media to teach leadership concepts can be especially powerful. Media have the ability to make complex concepts visible and make them come alive—a necessary but rare ingredient in successful leadership development efforts. In this chapter, we will present a pedagogical framework for using movies, television, literature, and music to teach leadership. First, though, an overview of current ideas on leadership is presented.

Understanding Leadership

In recent years, countless theories and models of leadership have been introduced. These include the Relational Leadership Model (Komives, Lucas, and McMahon, 1998), servant leadership (Greenleaf, 1977), situational leadership (Hersey, Blanchard, and Johnson, 2000), the Social Change Model of Leadership (Astin and Astin, 1995), systemic leadership (Allen and Cherrey, 2000), and transformational leadership (Burns, 1978). Leadership educators may use these theories and models singly or in combination, or they may embrace the use of habits (Covey, 1989), practices (Kouzes and Posner, 2002), learning organizations (Senge, 1990), or chaos (Wheatley, 1999).

This range of theories and models can be overwhelming for educators seeking *the* best approach and for students seeking *the* right answers to their questions about leadership. Since leadership occurs across many contexts and disciplines, it can be conceptualized differently from campus to campus and from department to department. Students need to understand that leadership is complex and multidimensional and that it cannot be reduced to simple charts or formulas. While this section is not intended to be exhaustive in covering the various ways to conceptualize leadership development in higher education, it does demonstrate the wide range of resources that can be used to supplement this discussion of using entertainment media to teach leadership.

Teaching Leadership

As previously stated, there are many models and theories of leadership. However, these are useful only to the extent that they provide a useful framework for actually getting down to the business of developing leadership in others. While it is necessary to be aware of the numerous ways to understand leadership, it is equally important to understand the various ways to teach leadership.

In the literature, definitions of leadership abound, and there is often disagreement among them. Because of this, the teaching of leadership often suffers; it is difficult to teach what is ill defined. Leadership development often tends to one of two extremes; either it is of the feel-good variety that produces positive feelings but little in the way of transferable skills, or it focuses on prescriptive formulas and models of specific skills, with little attention to context or the more esoteric aspects of leadership, such as diversity, ethics, or self-awareness. An effective approach to leadership development starts with clear objectives and specific desired outcomes.

Conceptualization of the intent and desired outcomes of the experience is the necessary first step in enhancing the learning of the participants. Using entertainment media to teach leadership lends itself to integrating these approaches if it is done in a proactive, thoughtful way. Thus, it is useful to consider models that can help conceptualize and design effective leadership development programs.

Intentions and Goals. Any development program can be thought of from three perspectives (Roberts, 1978):

1. Training: an intervention that helps someone become more effective in current tasks or positions (for example, teaching a residence hall leader how to motivate others more effectively).
2. Education: prepares someone for future activities or positions (for example, a future student government leader learning how to run a meeting).
3. Development: helps someone grow as a person and may or may not have a direct application to a current or future leadership role (for example, an Outward Bound experience).

As a guide to leadership development goals and activities, these perspectives provide a framework for choosing the specific medium to use, designing the activities around that medium, and directing the processing of the experience. It is always important to match the specific use of media to the goals of the experience or activity.

Experience and Process. Having determined the intent of the development experience, the session leader can then plan the process that will produce the desired outcomes. Kolb's experiential learning cycle (Kolb, 1984) provides an effective way to frame learning experiences and is suitable for planning the use of media to develop leadership. The model says that participants engage in an experience, process that experience, generalize learnings from the experience, and then apply those learnings to new situations. This process often produces the "aha" insights that can be so valuable in leadership development and lends itself especially well to activities based on the "Development" perspective mentioned in the preceding section, although it can also be used in the other areas.

Kolb's model (Kolb, 1984) works equally well for training students in a specific skill or educating them on a particular topic. The difference in these cases is that the experience is framed or set up in a specific way before the participant engages in the activity. The session leader might instruct participants to notice particular characteristics of their own or others' behavior or to watch specifically for a particular skill. The experience is then debriefed specifically within the frame that was provided beforehand. In this process, a particular outcome or skill is desired, whereas in the developmental process, participants are being asked to develop their own insights from the experience, whatever they may be.

With any experience, how and when the experience is processed, or debriefed, are critical. If the learning is not reinforced in a way that increases the chances of generalization or transfer of the skill to new situations, then the training is an isolated event with little value. Kolb's model (Kolb, 1984) provides a simple yet effective way to debrief an experience. Conceptually, it is set up like a funnel. Immediately following an experience, participants need help to sort out what happened, what they think, and what is important. Initially, the facilitator keeps the discussion broad, allowing participants to freely explore their own experience with little direction. As the debriefing progresses, the facilitator gradually narrows, or funnels, the discussion toward the issues that are key to the intent of the session or to the strong reactions of the participants.

Luckner and Nadler (1997) state that for true behavior change to occur, facilitators and participants must recognize that there are several choice points in the process of reflecting on experience, analyzing learning, and deciding how to respond in the future. In Luckner and Nadler's Levels of Processing model, the first stage, awareness, is designed to help the participant focus on the behaviors, thoughts, and experience of the here and now. The second stage, responsibility, allows participants to bridge how these behaviors, ideas, and experiences are similar to what they might do or experience elsewhere. At this stage, participants choose whether to do anything with their observations. If they choose to do so, they move to the third stage, experimentation, either in a subsequent activity or in a controlled situation; if not, they choose to stay the same. The assumption is that participants often make this choice internally, maybe even outside their own awareness; the intent here is to make the choice explicit. Finally, once experimentation has occurred and further reflection on the experiment has helped the participant make adjustments, the choice is made to either stay the same or transfer new ideas and behaviors to real situations in the participant's life (Luckner and Nadler, 1997).

While watching a movie or reading a piece of literature might seem like a passive activity, our contention is that media use in any teaching scenario should be viewed as an experiential activity. To ensure that media use in teaching is an active activity, we advocate the use of the experiential learning cycle and a structured processing model. By using these models, instructors become more proactive in planning their learning objectives and using activities that supplement the medium, and they are more focused and targeted in their processing of the activity.

Using Movies to Teach Leadership

It is not enough to show a movie and ask, "What do you think?" More planning will enhance the use of media as a tool for meaningful learning and behavioral change. One way to begin thinking about how to use entertainment media to teach leadership is to examine an example. Consider the film *Sister Act* (1992). Following is a brief summary of the plot:

Sister Mary Clarence (Whoopi Goldberg) is actually a lounge singer named Deloris who is living in a convent as part of a witness protection program. In the convent, she takes on the role of choir director and demonstrates many leadership skills to inspire and raise the performance of the current choir, which is not very good.

This movie provides opportunities to explore many topics and provides examples of women in leadership, a subject that is often not considered in leadership development.

Using *Sister Act* to teach leadership development requires some planning. It can be viewed in its entirety, or specific scenes can be used to illustrate specific topics. Following are some examples of potential leadership topics illustrated by specific segments of the film:

- Complimenting before giving feedback. (Sister Mary Clarence compliments Sister Mary Patrick on her powerful voice before she asks her to sing more softly.)
- Empowering others. (Sister Mary Clarence helps Sister Mary Robert realize that she can sing louder and well.)

- Getting people to work together. (Sister Mary Clarence stresses the importance of choir members' listening to one another.)
- Providing inspiration. (Sister Mary Clarence tells the choir members that they are "singing to the Lord.")
- Risk taking. (Sister Mary Clarence has the choir try something new and daring—an upbeat version of a traditional hymn.)

As a simple example, consider the scene that demonstrates "complimenting before giving feedback." As a facilitator, this scene is ideal for training on feedback skills for current student leaders. For use in training, the scene might be preceded by a mini-lecture on constructive feedback. This format allows students to know what they are looking for when watching the scene. For example, consider the scene in which Sister Mary Clarence compliments Sister Mary Patrick on her powerful voice before she asks her to sing more softly.

In the context of the experiential learning cycle, the students have now had an experience—that is, watching the clip and looking for specific traits in the movie. In the debriefing, students are asked to identify specific behaviors that demonstrate effective feedback. Using the processing model previously discussed, the students are aware of the desired behavior. They must then link that behavior to their own experience in the responsibility stage. The debriefing thus moves to a discussion of how this behavior is similar to what they might do elsewhere in their lives.

Next, the participants choose to further practice giving feedback in the experimentation stage.

In this stage, the facilitator provides more specific training in the form of a lecture and then sets up opportunities to practice through role plays or other activities. The participants then debrief their experimentation: What worked? What did not? What was difficult? What adjustments need to be made?

To conclude this activity, the facilitator leads a discussion on how to transfer these skills into participants' everyday activities. This discussion allows participants to explore other choices, such as whether they are willing to try these new behaviors. If they are, commitment has been gained, and action plans for implementing these behaviors are developed.

In the preceding example, a compelling experience has been designed around one movie scene. If one considers the entire movie or scenes from several different movies, the possibilities are myriad. The entire film *Sister Act* could serve as a foundation for a leadership series that addresses many skills. Also, scenes could be gathered from several movies that show various aspects of one skill set, such as giving feedback. Exhibit 6.1 shows the process of planning an activity that uses an entertainment medium; this example uses the movie *Apollo 13* (1995), which provides many obvious yet evocative examples of leadership skills in action.

Exhibit 6.1. Activity Planning Template

Process Steps	Activity Plan
Determine intent	To facilitate student learning about activity teams and team-based problem solving
Choose medium to use	Film: *Apollo 13*
	Scene: The engineers realize that there is a problem with the carbon monoxide levels in the capsule. It ends with the engineers gathering materials to fix the problem.
Frame the experience	Frame the experience of watching the media clip with a discussion about teams and teamwork. Instruct students to note specific behaviors that either helped or hindered the team process.
Engage in the experience	Watch the video clip.
Process the experience	Debrief the scene:
1. Awareness	What is happening in this scene with regard to teamwork? What's working? What's not? In what ways are the behaviors in the video similar to your own experiences with teams?
2. Responsibility	How can you apply what you saw in the video to your future experiences with teams? Are you willing to try these new behaviors in your teams?
3. Experimentation	Engage participants in a practice activity to try new behaviors, or have participants develop a plan of action to try new behaviors. After experimentation, participants should then decide whether and how these new behaviors should be applied in their future activities.

Using Television to Teach Leadership

Next, we will discuss using television to teach leadership. As might be expected, the process is much the same, but it is helpful to consider a specific example.

Many television series contain examples of leadership. While few television series have dealt directly with college students (with the notable exceptions of *Beverly Hills 90210* and *Felicity*), many have addressed leadership.

Using television shows to teach leadership follows the same general pattern as using movies. Whether you are using one scene or the entire show, the key to student learning is the processing that happens afterward. The Activity Planning Template (Exhibit 6.1) can also be used with television shows.

A television series that is filled with examples of various perspectives on leadership is *M*A*S*H* (1972–1983). This award-winning show follows the exploits of unforgettable characters in a Mobile Army Surgical Hospital unit (MASH 4077) during the Korean War. An episode that can serve as a springboard to a multifaceted discussion of leadership is "Change of Command"

(1975), which is available on DVD. Following is a summary of the plot of the episode: Major Frank Burns has assumed the leadership of the unit following the departure and subsequent death of beloved Colonel Henry Blake. Burns believes in doing things "by the book" and, with the support of head nurse Major Margaret Houlihan, hopes to make things "right" in the unit, correcting what he sees as problems with the lax leadership style of Blake. Unfortunately for Burns, the army command has assigned Colonel Sherman Potter to lead the MASH unit—news that Burns does not take too well.

Potter arrives to take command, and changes begin immediately, starting with how he wants the office arranged. He meets and quickly reviews the files of the staff: Major Houlihan, Captains "Hawkeye" Pierce and B. J. Hunnicut, Father Francis Mulcahey, Corporals "Radar" O'Reilly and Max Klinger. (Major Burns has run away and will return later in the episode.) The unit soon receives a group of wounded soldiers and must provide medical care. Pierce is worried that Potter might not be a good surgeon but the new commander turns out to be very skilled, even helping Hunnicut with a tricky medical procedure. The episode ends with Potter, Hawkeye, and B. J. drinking, singing, and getting to know one another in the captains' tent.

While almost every show in the *M*A*S*H* series offers some unique perspective on leadership, this particular episode centers on the theme of change. It shows how members of an organization can react to a change in leadership and what it is like to be the new person—new to an organization and new to a leadership role in that organization. Among the different leadership lessons in this episode are the following:

- Dealing with disappointment as a leader. (Major Burns assumes he will be made the company commander. When that does not happen, he becomes upset and runs away.)
- Change from the perspective of the new leader. (Colonel Potter begins his new command by rearranging the office to fit his wants and needs and then meeting his staff.)
- Change from the perspective of the organization's participants. (Hawkeye and others loved Colonel Blake and are worried that Potter will not be a good surgeon or a good leader.)
- Proving yourself as a new leader. (Potter demonstrates to the unit that he is a good surgeon and not as "by the book" as they might have believed.)
- Working with different personalities within the organization. (Max Klinger, in a dress, barges into Potter's office and tells the commander that he's unfit for duty and should be discharged. Potter has seen this all before and tells Klinger to get out and get into a uniform.)
- Bending the rules. (Later in the episode, on the advice of the captains, Potter lets Klinger continue to wear dresses.)
- Getting to know the members of the organization. (After surgery, Potter bonds with Pierce and Hunnicut by drinking, singing, and telling stories.)

This episode can also be analyzed using Kolb's experiential learning cycle (Kolb, 1984) or the "levels of processing" model (Luckner and Nadler, 1997). While some viewers will probably know the characters, others should be told that the setting is the Korean War and that the previous commander (Blake) departed a short while ago. The show combines elements of humor and drama in a way that makes watching it an engaging experience.

Using Popular Books to Teach Leadership

Many classic works of literature can be used to teach leadership (Mayer and Clemens, 1999), but using popular books may seem to make little sense, given the huge number of volumes published each year that focus directly on the topic. However, both fiction and nonfiction books can help students better understand the complex subject of leadership. These books, such as *Lord of the Flies* (Golding, 1954), *Tuesdays with Morrie* (Albom, 1997), *To Kill a Mockingbird* (Lee, 1960), and *Dead Man Walking* (Prejean, 1993) are widely available or easily ordered, are reasonable in price, and are engaging to readers. Because books that address leadership themes are numerous, each student in a class can select a different book and share what he or she learned, thus producing a collective effect far beyond what might have occurred if everyone read the same work.

A typical way to use popular press books is to have students read different books, complete a written assignment detailing what they learned about leadership, and make short class reports about the books. The books can be selected entirely by the students or selected or assigned from a list provided by the instructor. Giving students some choice in the matter is obviously preferable, to give them a chance to choose something they find engaging. The books can be fiction or nonfiction and can include biographies of specific leaders. One key point that needs reinforcing, especially if the students read biographies, is that their written and oral reports are not to focus entirely on the factual events outlined in the book but more on what the student learned about leadership from reading it. Assignments such as this one provide students an excuse to read books that they have been wanting to read but have not had a chance to read yet.

This assignment can also provide an opportunity for students to explore their passions, perhaps by selecting a work of science fiction or fantasy or reading a biography of a personal hero. Connecting the personal passions of students to the subject of leadership can result in interesting papers and reports and enhanced learning.

Using Music to Teach Leadership

Students encounter music every day; therefore, it is a medium with great potential as a media tool to teach leadership, although its use is not as straightforward as the use of movies, television, or books. Music serves as a wonderful metaphor for leadership and is a medium that allows strong emotions to emerge. Individuals can use music to show differences in how leadership is conceptualized by asking the following questions: How is leadership like classical music? Jazz? Country music? Rap? Hip hop? Pop? John Kao (1997) uses "Take Five" by the Dave Brubeck Quartet as a wonderful example of why "constancy" and "artistry" are both important in leadership and organizations. One without the other is incomplete.

Music can be used in many ways in a leadership class or a workshop setting. Student leaders can explore diversity issues through music by identifying and comparing favorite artists—thus showing the wide range of musical tastes that can exist in a seemingly homogeneous group. Students can select specific pieces of music as theme songs for groups or teams or to exemplify different aspects of leadership. Finally, music can be used to enhance the mood within a learning environment. Whether quiet reflection or raucous energy is desired, music can be an invaluable tool in making the space more conducive and the audience more receptive to what will happen next. The full potential of music to enhance the teaching and learning of leadership has yet to be realized, so feel free to experiment.

Conclusion

This chapter is meant to be a guide. By presenting a pedagogical framework for working with media to teach leadership, we hope to provide a starting point for those who are helping to develop student leaders. In addition, we hope that this framework will enhance the students' experience and strengthen their learning. However, like any good model or theory, the framework is meant to be suggestive rather than prescriptive. Experiment. Break the rules. Try something new. After all, that *is* experiential learning.

References

Albom, M. *Tuesdays with Morrie: An Old Man, a Young Man, and Life's Greatest Lesson.* New York: Doubleday, 1997.

Allen, K. E., and Cherrey, C. *Systemic Leadership: Enriching the Meaning of Our Work.* Lanham, Md.: University Press of America, 2000.

Apollo 13 [motion picture]. United States: Universal Studios, 1995.

Astin, A., and Astin, H. *Social Change Model of Leadership Development.* Los Angeles: Higher Education Leadership Institute, University of California, Los Angeles, 1995.

Burns, J. M. *Leadership.* New York: HarperCollins, 1978.

"Change of Command" [television series episode]. M*A*S*H. United States: Twentieth Century Fox Home Entertainment, 1975.

Covey, S. R. *The Seven Habits of Highly Effective People.* New York: Simon & Schuster, 1989.

Golding, W. R. *Lord of the Flies.* London: Faber and Faber, 1954.

Greenleaf, R. *Servant Leadership: A Journey into the Nature of Legitimate Power and Greatness.* Ramsey, N.J.: Paulist Press, 1977.

Hersey, P., Blanchard, K. H., and Johnson, D. E. *Management of Organizational Behavior: Leading Human Resources.* (8th ed.) Upper Saddle River, N.J.: Prentice Hall, 2000.

Kao, J. *Jamming: The Art and Discipline of Corporate Creativity.* New York: Harper-Business, 1997.

Kolb, D. A. *Experiential Learning: Experience as the Source of Learning and Development.* Englewood Cliffs, N.J.: Prentice Hall, 1984.

Komives, S. R., Lucas, N., and McMahon, T. R. *Exploring Leadership: For College Students Who Want to Make a Difference.* San Francisco: Jossey-Bass, 1998.

Kouzes, J. M., and Posner, B. Z. *The Leadership Challenge: How to Get Extraordinary Things Done in Organizations.* (3rd ed.) San Francisco: Jossey-Bass, 2002.

Lee, H. *To Kill a Mockingbird.* Philadelphia: Lippincott, 1960.

Luckner, J. L., and Nadler, R. S. *Processing the Experience: Strategies to Enhance and Generalize Learning.* (2nd ed.) Dubuque, Iowa: Kendall/Hunt, 1997.

M*A*S*H [television series]. United States: Twentieth Century Fox Home Entertainment, 1972–1983.

Mayer, D. F., and Clemens, J. K. *The Classic Touch: Lessons in Leadership from Homer to Hemingway.* New York: McGraw-Hill, 1999.

Prejean, H. *Dead Man Walking: An Eyewitness Account of the Death Penalty in the United States.* New York: Random House, 1993.

Roberts, D. C. (ed.). *Student Leadership Programs in Higher Education.* Washington, D.C.: American College Personnel Association, 1978.

Senge, P. *The Fifth Discipline: The Art and Practice of the Learning Organization.* New York: Doubleday, 1990.

Sister Act [motion picture]. United States: Touchstone Pictures, 1992.

Wheatley, M. J. *Leadership and the New Science.* (2nd ed.) San Francisco: Berrett-Koehler, 1999.

TIMOTHY R. MCMAHON *is a faculty consultant in the Teaching Effectiveness Program at the University of Oregon, Eugene.*

RON BRAMHALL *is a leadership and communication instructor in the Lundquist College of Business at the University of Oregon, Eugene.*

Ways to use films, television programs, popular music, and popular books to teach counseling skills are described.

Using Entertainment Media to Inform Student Affairs Teaching and Practice Related to Counseling Skills

Deborah J. Taub, Deanna S. Forney

Most student affairs master's students do not seek to become licensed professional counselors; however, developing a foundation in counseling skills has long been considered an important part of the professional preparation of student affairs professionals. Counseling has been called "one of the cornerstone skills" (Gilmore, 1987, p. 296) of the student affairs profession. Edmund G. Williamson, dean of students at the University of Minnesota in the 1930s, was an early articulator of the counseling role of student affairs; Williamson believed that "the counseling approach is universally applicable to the various functions of the student services worker, providing a core from which all of these services can develop" (Betz, 1987, p. 176).

The importance of counseling skills is recognized in the standards for master's level professional preparation in student affairs published by the Council for the Advancement of Standards in Higher Education (CAS). The foundational studies curricular standards, under "Individual, Group, and Organizational Intervention," call for "substantial instruction in counseling and group dynamics" (Miller, 2003).

The student affairs profession makes substantial use of undergraduate student paraprofessionals in program and service delivery to students in higher education through positions such as resident assistants (RAs), orientation assistants, and peer mentors, peer advisers, or peer counselors (Ender, 1984). Their training frequently includes counseling skills designed to enhance their ability to act as "helpers/facilitators" (Winston and Fitch, 1993,

p. 326). RAs, for example, may attempt to help roommates work through conflicts, and orientation leaders aid new students in their initial adjustment to college, including helping with possible feelings of homesickness. Winston and Fitch report that acting in a helping capacity is seen as an important part of the RA role by RAs, faculty, staff, students, and parents.

Authors have recommended training in counseling and helping skills for paraprofessionals in residence life (Blimling, 1999; Winston and Fitch, 1993), orientation (Ender and Strumpf, 1984), academic advising (Habley, 1984), and counseling and career centers (Delworth and Johnson, 1984). The goal is to equip paraprofessionals with the skills necessary to facilitate the development of relationships and rapport and to serve in a helping capacity.

Basic counseling skills to be learned are generally grounded in one of the major training approaches (for example, Egan, 2002; Ivey and Ivey, 2003). Skills to be learned include attending, active listening, reflection, probing, summarizing, goal setting, and action planning (Egan, 2002; Habley, 1984).

Use of Entertainment Media in Counseling Training

Teaching and learning counseling skills is a time-intensive process, a fact that is acknowledged in the CAS standards' requirement for extensive practice, supervision, and feedback (Miller, 2003). Ender (1984) recommends a minimum of 40 hours of counseling skill training for paraprofessionals. Trainees (whether graduate students in student affairs or undergraduate paraprofessionals) must learn, practice, and refine a number of new skills. Many of these skills may seem awkward, artificial, or mechanical to "helpers in training" (Egan, 2002). Some trainees may view the skills training as unnecessary, because they consider themselves natural helpers or born counselors. Many state, "I'm the one my friends always come to with their problems."

Furthermore, it can be difficult for trainees to understand how the various skills are to be integrated in practice. Egan (2002) describes the following steps in the training process: (1) cognitive understanding, (2) clarification, (3) modeling, (4) written exercises, (5) practice, (6) feedback, (7) evaluating the learning process, and (8) supervised practice with actual clients. According to Egan, steps 1–6 lead to initial competence, and the remaining steps lead to initial mastery.

Counseling training frequently makes use of videotapes to provide models of the counseling process in action. Typically, these video models are in the form of training tapes that accompany texts (such as the videotape that accompanies Murphy and Dillon's *Interviewing in Action* [2003]) or one or more of the generally available classic training tapes (for example, "Gloria" from *Three Approaches to Psychotherapy*, 1965). Although such tapes can be effective, they also present a number of potential problems for trainers and trainees.

Yager, Johns, Ingram, and Brown (1995) found that recognized or "known" therapists were rated by trainees as more "expert, attractive, and trustworthy" (p. 9) than unfamiliar or "unknown" therapists in the same clinical interactions; therefore, they recommended against the use of commercially available videos in favor of role-play demonstrations by instructors known to the students. The language, clothing, and hairstyles captured in videotapes can be distracting to students and may undermine the credibility of the tape for some students. (In recent classes, our students have pointed out "outdated haircuts" such as "mullets," "prehistoric" Apple computers, and "pouf" skirts while watching videos in class.) Because training videos are expensive, however, libraries and administrators frequently are unwilling to retire and replace videos quickly enough to keep the trends and fads depicted up to date.

In addition, the expert models presented in many training videos may seem too perfect to students; they may perceive the gap between their own skill level and that of the expert as simply too great to be bridged. Finally, students find many of the available training videos boring.

Examples of Entertainment Media Use from the Classroom and the Training Room

Many examples from films, television programs, music, and popular books that can be adapted for course and workshop use are presented here.

Movies and Television Shows. The use of entertainment media such as feature films and television shows can be an effective technique in counseling training. The literature contains many examples of recommendations for the use of films in teaching counseling-related content. Use of films may aid instructors in increasing counselor empathic responses (Gladstein and Feldstein, 1983) and teaching group counseling (Tyler and Reynolds, 1998). Watching films can help students grasp counseling theories (Koch and Dollarhide, 2000), understand mental disorders (Hyler, 1988; Wedding and Boyd, 1999), and improve client self-understanding (Hesley and Hesley, 1998).

One concern about the use of feature films and television programs in counseling training might be the unrealistic and often unflattering portrayal of counselors, psychologists, psychiatrists, and other professional helpers common to these genres (categories that frequently are not distinctly differentiated in the media). Behavior that helping professionals widely consider to be unethical (such as becoming sexually involved with a client or gossiping about a client with friends and family) seems to be de rigueur among Hollywood's helpers (see, for example, The Prince of Tides, 1991; The Evening Star, 1996; Basic Instinct, 1992; Tin Cup, 1996; and What About Bob? 1991). In fact, scenes from The Prince of Tides have been used in classes on professional ethics to illustrate unethical and potentially illegal behavior on the part of a therapist (Hesley and Hesley, 1998).

· Also of concern are portrayals of helpers as either incompetent or overly competent. Diefenbach, Burns, and Schwartz (1998) found that one week of prime-time television contained several portrayals of mental health professionals as incompetent and several portrayals of mental health professionals as "wonder workers." The image of the bumbling helper is common in the movies and on television. While some students may feel that this characterization belittles counselors, the ineffective helper image and behavior can be used to provoke discussion about the pros and cons of the character's approach as well as how students might approach the helping situation differently. The "wonder worker" characterizations, though not demeaning, are troublesome because of the ways in which they may make the counselor seem superhuman and because of the unrealistic expectations of counseling that they may implant. It is important to address directly with students any concerns about the depiction of counselors that are raised by the use of popular films and television shows. Such portrayals can serve as catalysts for discussion of ethical issues, people's expectations of counseling, and reasons that people do and do not seek counseling.

The examples of film and television show use that follow are intended as aids in teaching basic counseling concepts and skills to student affairs master's students and undergraduate students who may be enrolled in formal courses or who may be receiving more limited exposure through vehicles such as staff training and peer helper education. The choice of film and television clips should be geared to the depth of exposure that students will receive. For example, comedic portrayals rather than more in-depth treatments may be more helpful in cases of short-term exposure, such as staff training and peer education. Similarly, portrayals of professional therapists may be more appropriate for graduate students enrolled in formal counseling coursework.

Short clips from movies and television shows can be used to demonstrate specific concepts and techniques related to counseling and helping. The anxiety and reluctance that individuals may feel (as well as the potential ulterior motives) when seeking professional help for the first time are depicted in a humorous but insightful way in *Tin Cup* (1996) when the lead character, played by Kevin Costner, decides to go see a counselor in hopes of gaining her assistance in figuring out how he might go about asking her out. Rene Russo, playing the therapist, provokes laughter with her rather ineffective approach. The humor in such scenarios can also aid students in overcoming their own self-consciousness when doing practice role plays, tapes, and so on.

Similarly, Billy Crystal's portrayal of the therapist in *Analyze This* (1999) provides an example of his fantasy reaction to a whining client. Only in his head does he say what he really thinks of her, an example of how not to confront. The appropriateness of filters and the ability to rise above one's own reactions to individuals that one needs to serve in a helping role are discussion topics that can emerge from such comedic portrayals.

Clips from *Dead Poets Society* (1989) can be used to illustrate the importance of listening to the client and the pitfalls of giving advice. When Neil's father orders Neil to give up acting, Neil turns to his teacher, John Keating, for support. Hesley and Hesley (1998) call *Dead Poets Society* "an illustration of what *not* to do" (p. 156); Keating, without fully understanding the family dynamics involved, gives advice instead of offering support. Feeling hopeless, Neil ultimately commits suicide.

The television series *Ally McBeal* (1997–2002) often used guest stars (for example, Tracy Ullman, Bruce Willis, Rosie O'Donnell, and Betty White) as therapists. Clips in which the therapists' unorthodox techniques are demonstrated can be used to stimulate discussion about effective and ineffective helping strategies and alternate approaches to the ones seen on screen.

Several media representations that reflect the helping process from a more serious perspective are also available. *The Sopranos* television series (1999–2004) is one example. *The Sopranos* provides many examples of counseling scenes, especially between the lead character, Tony Soprano, and his therapist, Dr. Jennifer Melfi.

The first episode of the series ("The Sopranos," 1999) is especially useful. The entire episode is framed by Tony's conversations with Dr. Melfi. Unlike many portrayals of therapists in the media (Gabbard and Gabbard, 1987), Dr. Melfi is presented as a competent but humanly flawed practitioner. The episode opens with Tony talking with Dr. Melfi for the first time. He comes to therapy because he is experiencing panic attacks. Flashbacks to the actual situations that Tony describes serve to reinforce or contradict the representation he gives to Dr. Melfi. Watching the entire episode, including pausing to process with the students what they see and hear happening in each counseling-related segment, provides a holistic look at the counseling process and an opportunity to discuss techniques, pros and cons of the therapist's performance, ethical issues, and so forth. For example, Tony sometimes distorts the events he describes; Dr. Melfi clarifies ethical and legal boundaries; Tony pushes for a premature termination of therapy, displaying approach/avoidance issues in regard to seeking and receiving help; counselor and client run into each other at a restaurant; and Dr. Melfi prescribes Prozac for Tony.

While the portrayal of the counseling process in *The Sopranos* has been praised by professional practitioners for its authenticity (Gabbard, 2002), some scenes, such as those containing violence, can be difficult to watch. Student viewers should be cautioned, and student reactions should be processed. With some clips, it may be appropriate to give students the option not to watch.

In introducing counseling/helping models to students, it is typical to teach and demonstrate each stage and skill as an individual component of the process. While this approach certainly has value in affording students an opportunity to fully examine and grasp concepts and learn how to demonstrate skills, examples of putting all the pieces together are also needed to aid students in conceptualizing about when and how to use such models and techniques.

The film *Good Will Hunting* (1997) provides another example of a therapist who is portrayed as competent but humanly flawed. The eight therapy segments, when viewed in succession (deleting the intervening portions of the film), afford an opportunity to watch a counseling process over time, to put the pieces together, and to recognize stages as they unfold and skills as they are employed. After each segment, students can be asked to identify what they think is occurring and why, techniques being used, what they would have done similarly and differently, and ethical issues raised. If deemed necessary, important plot points occurring between sessions can be shared verbally by the instructor or students who have seen the film.

Will Hunting is a math whiz who has relationship and anger management issues stemming from childhood abuse. Several therapists have been unsuccessful in their attempts to work with him. Some examples of techniques used and ethical issues raised in the clips include the new therapist, Sean Maguire, grabbing Will by the throat during the first session; Will demonstrating resistance in the third session by sitting silently for the entire time; Sean starting to fall asleep in the fourth session; Will's resistance gradually giving way as he asks Sean questions in the fifth session; Sean kicking Will out in the sixth session when he refuses to be serious; Sean and Will experiencing an emotional breakthrough in the seventh session; and closure in the eighth session. Sean's patience, self-disclosure, and ability to both challenge and support Will permeate the process.

The film *Ordinary People* (1980) can be used in much the same way, stopping for discussion after each therapy scene. *Ordinary People* provides another excellent depiction of the counseling process and features several scenes between Dr. Berger and his adolescent client Conrad that show the unfolding of the counseling process. Conrad's problems and concerns are developmentally typical of late adolescents (management of emotions, difficulties in friendships and relationships, conflict with parents), which makes this film well suited to an audience of future student affairs professionals (and potentially to an audience of undergraduate paraprofessionals). While the dated nature of the cars, hairstyles, and fashions might be distracting to students, the counseling process scenes contain less of this kind of distracting detail and work well in isolation from the rest of the film.

A potential problem with both *Good Will Hunting* (1997) and *Ordinary People* (1980) is that in both films, the therapist and the client are white men. A more multicultural alternative is *Antwone Fisher* (2002), which depicts the arc of a therapeutic relationship between a black male therapist and a black male client. Fisher's presenting problem, anger management, and his history of childhood abuse, which is revealed as his therapy unfolds, are similar to those of Will Hunting. *Antwone Fisher* provides opportunities to discuss mandatory counseling, client resistance, time-limited therapy, bibliotherapy, advice giving, boundaries, and counselor self-disclosure.

In training undergraduate paraprofessional helpers (resident assistants, orientation assistants, peer mentors, and the like), scenes from the television series *Felicity* (1998–2001) may be more appropriate than some of the films previously discussed. The scenarios encountered and the types of helping portrayed in *Felicity* are more similar to paraprofessionals' situations than the intense therapist-client relationships portrayed in *Good Will Hunting* or *The Sopranos*.

The pilot episode ("Pilot," 1998) and the episode "Boggled" (1998) include several scenes between new first-year student Felicity Porter and her sophomore RA, Noel, at the fictional University of New York. "The Last Stand" (1998) shows Noel dealing, not so successfully, with a roommate conflict and with the parents of a resident. The episode can be stopped periodically, and students can be asked to identify what Noel is doing well and poorly and how they might have responded. "Boggled" also raises ethical issues about relationships between RAs and residents and about the use and misuse of power and privilege as Noel circumvents procedure to give Felicity a refrigerator because he is romantically interested in her. Considering the impact of these issues on residents can spark discussion. The pilot episode and "The Last Stand" also feature useful scenes of Felicity and her academic adviser that can be used in a similar way. If clips and scenes are used rather than entire hour-long episodes, students may need to be filled in on the basics of the story line and the complex relationships between the characters.

The "Boggled" episode can also be used in the counseling classroom or in in-service training to illustrate the concept of dual relationships. This episode powerfully dramatizes the impact of the dual relationship between Noel and Felicity (as RA and resident and as romantic interests) and the impact of others' perceptions of the nature of their relationship on Felicity herself and on the other residents of the floor. Students can discuss the variety of feelings that are generated (anger, betrayal, jealousy, suspicion, and so on) and the consequences of the dual relationship. They also can discuss how Noel might have handled the situation better or how they might handle a similar situation. Students also can be asked to role-play the various floor residents as they interact with Felicity and with Noel.

Films and television shows have teaching and training applications beyond serving as discussion starters. Another use of films or television shows in counseling training is as the stimulus for papers or exams. Students can be asked to identify such things as skills or techniques being used and stages of counseling portrayed or to write about how they might proceed if they were the counselor. For example, an introductory group counseling course used *Dead Poets Society* (1989) as the stimulus for the final exam; students were asked to identify the stages of group development, discuss group leadership as portrayed in the film, and identify counseling issues portrayed.

Popular Music. Popular music can be used to set a tone, such as playing "Help!" (Lennon and McCartney, 2000) by the Beatles at the start of the first meeting of a graduate counseling course, when students may be nervous about the nature of the course. Music can also promote understanding and retention of important concepts by both graduate and undergraduate students. For example, music can be used in teaching Egan's helping model (Egan, 2002), to promote easy retention of the basic focus of each stage. For stage one of the model, the emphasis is on exploration. Marvin Gaye's "What's Going On" (Cleveland, Gaye, and Benson, 2000) or the Beatles' "What Goes On" (Lennon, McCartney, and Starr, 1990) forms an easy connection. Stage two, which focuses on goal setting, can be represented by the Spice Girls' "Wannabe" (1996); the lyrics ask the listener to indicate what he or she wants. Finally, stage three, which emphasizes moving to action, can be symbolized by Elvis Presley's "A Little Less Conversation" (Strange and Davis, 2002), with its plea for moving from talking to acting.

The song "You've Got a Friend" (King, 2003) also can be used to set the stage for the introduction of counseling skills; it introduces the idea of needing someone else's help. The same song can be used as a springboard for a discussion of the differences between being a counselor and being a friend. For more advanced students, such a discussion might also include a clip from the final therapy session between Dr. Berger and Conrad in *Ordinary People* (1980), in which Dr. Berger says that he is Conrad's friend.

Berk (2002, 2003) provides extensive discussion and detailed examples of other uses of music in the classroom. Berk recommends music as one way to bring humor into the classroom and to connect with the emotions of students.

Popular Books. Popular books can provide another enjoyable way for students to learn about counseling. Although psychotherapy has been a popular subject for novels and memoirs, choosing appropriate books for student affairs counseling trainees and undergraduate peer counselors can be difficult. Many of the available popular books concern severe pathology and focus more on the experience of hospitalization than on the counseling process (for example, *Girl, Interrupted* [Kaysen, 1993], *I Never Promised You a Rose Garden* [Greenberg, 1964], *One Flew Over the Cuckoo's Nest* [Kesey, 1962]).

Yalom's humorous novel *Lying on the Couch* (1996) portrays several therapists and clients throughout the counseling process. The novel provides students with a view of different counseling orientations in action, shows the stages of the counseling process, and presents a variety of intriguing ethical issues for discussion.

Group: Six People in Search of a Life (Solotaroff, 1999) is journalist Solotaroff's account of the process and progress of a counseling group of which he was a member. *Group* provides an excellent illustration of the stages of group development; it also provides an opportunity to discuss group leadership issues.

Popular books also can help students develop greater understanding of problems such as depression (for example, *Darkness Visible* [Styron, 1990]), bipolar disorder (*An Unquiet Mind* [Jamison, 1995]), self-injury ("cutting") (*Skin Game* [Kettlewell, 1999]), eating disorders (*Wasted* [Hornbacher, 1998]), and suicide (*The Tender Land* [Finneran, 2000]). (These books are, of course, only a few of the books available on these topics.) A word of caution should be noted: these books offer intimate and graphic looks at these problems that students may find disturbing, particularly if they have had personal experiences with similar situations.

In any case, popular books such as these require a much greater investment of time on the part of students than do any of the other media discussed in this chapter. This logistical fact, coupled with the advanced nature of the content, makes such books appropriate for graduate-level formal coursework rather than undergraduate training or training workshops. The books can be used as supplemental reading. Deb Taub has had success in forming students into "book groups" to discuss and present on their supplemental books.

Conclusion

Films, television shows, popular music, and popular books can be effective tools for teaching counseling skills. There are a number of benefits to using popular media. Students with a variety of learning styles respond well to media use, and it can help students synthesize the disparate parts of counseling skills and the counseling process to see the whole picture. Use of entertainment media can also aid in the retention of key concepts and bring interest, humor, and drama into the classroom.

References

Ally McBeal [television series]. United States: Twentieth Century Fox Television, 1997–2002.
Analyze This [motion picture]. United States: Warner Brothers, 1999.
Antwone Fisher [motion picture]. United States: Twentieth Century Fox Films, 2002.
Basic Instinct [motion picture]. United States: TriStar Pictures, 1992.
Berk, R. A. *Humor as an Instructional Defibrillator*. Sterling, Va.: Stylus, 2002.
Berk, R. A. *Professors Are from Mars, Students Are from Snickers*. Sterling, Va.: Stylus, 2003.
Betz, E. "The Counselor Role." In U. Delworth and G. R. Hanson (eds.), *Student Services: A Handbook for the Profession*. San Francisco: Jossey-Bass, 1987.
Blimling, G. *The Resident Assistant*. (5th ed.) Dubuque, Iowa: Kendall/Hunt, 1999.
"Boggled" [television series episode]. *Felicity*. United States: Buena Vista Entertainment, 1998.
Cleveland, A., Gaye, M., and Benson, R. "What's Going On" [Recorded by Marvin Gaye]. CD, *Every Great Motown Hit*. United States: The Universal/Motown Records Group, 2000 (recorded 1971).
Dead Poets Society [motion picture]. United States: Touchstone Pictures, 1989.
Delworth, U., and Johnson, M. M. "Student Paraprofessionals in Counseling and Career Centers." In S. C. Ender and R. B. Winston, Jr. (eds.), *Students as Paraprofessional Staff*. San Francisco: Jossey-Bass, 1984.

Diefenbach, D. L., Burns, N. J., and Schwartz, A. L. "Mental Health Professionals According to Prime-Time: An Explanatory Analysis." Paper presented at the American Psychological Association Annual Convention, San Francisco, 1998.

Egan, G. *The Skilled Helper*. (7th ed.) Pacific Grove, Calif.: Brooks/Cole, 2002.

Ender, K. L., and Strumpf, G. "Orientation and the Role of the Student Paraprofessional." In S. C. Ender and R. B. Winston, Jr. (eds.), *Students as Paraprofessional Staff*. San Francisco: Jossey-Bass, 1984.

Ender, S. C. "Student Paraprofessionals Within Student Affairs: The State of the Art." In S. C. Ender and R. B. Winston, Jr. (eds.), *Students as Paraprofessional Staff*. San Francisco: Jossey-Bass, 1984.

The Evening Star [motion picture]. United States: Paramount Pictures, 1996.

Felicity [television series]. United States, Buena Vista Entertainment, 1998–2001.

Finneran, K. *The Tender Land: A Family Love Story*. New York: Houghton Mifflin, 2000.

Gabbard, G. *The Psychology of The Sopranos: Love, Desire, and Betrayal in America's Favorite Gangster Family*. New York: Basic Books, 2002.

Gabbard, K., and Gabbard, G. O. *Psychiatry and the Cinema*. Chicago: University of Chicago Press, 1987.

Gilmore, S. K. "Counseling." In U. Delworth and G. R. Hanson (eds.), *Student Services: A Handbook for the Profession*. San Francisco: Jossey-Bass, 1987.

Gladstein, G. A., and Feldstein, J. C. "Using Film to Increase Counselor Empathic Experiences." *Counselor Education and Supervision*, 1983, 23(2), 125–131.

Good Will Hunting [motion picture]. United States: Miramax Films, 1997.

Greenberg, J. *I Never Promised You a Rose Garden*. New York: New American Library, 1964.

Habley, W. R. "Student Paraprofessionals in Academic Advising." In S. C. Ender and R. B. Winston, Jr. (eds.), *Students as Paraprofessional Staff*. San Francisco: Jossey-Bass, 1984.

Hesley, J. W., and Hesley, J. G. *Rent Two Films and Let's Talk in the Morning: Using Popular Movies in Psychotherapy*. New York: Wiley, 1998.

Hornbacher, M. *Wasted: A Memoir of Anorexia and Bulimia*. New York: HarperCollins, 1998.

Hyler, S. E. "DSM-III at the Cinema: Madness in the Movies." *Comprehensive Psychiatry*, 1988, 29(2), 195–206.

Ivey, A. E., and Ivey, M. B. *Intentional Interviewing and Counseling: Facilitating Client Development in a Multicultural Society*. Pacific Grove, Calif.: Brooks/Cole, 2003.

Jamison, K. R. *An Unquiet Mind*. New York: Vintage, 1995.

Kaysen, S. *Girl, Interrupted*. New York: Turtle Bay Books, 1993.

Kesey, K. *One Flew over the Cuckoo's Nest*. New York: New American Library, 1962.

Kettlewell, C. *Skin Game*. New York: St. Martin's Press, 1999.

King, C. "You've Got a Friend." [Recorded by James Taylor]. CD, *The Best of James Taylor*. United States: Warner Brothers, 2003 (recorded 1971).

Koch, G., and Dollarhide, C. T. "Using a Popular Film in Counselor Education: *Good Will Hunting* as a Teaching Tool." *Counselor Education and Supervision*, 2000, 39(3), 203–210.

"The Last Stand" [television series episode]. *Felicity*. United States: Buena Vista Entertainment, 1998.

Lennon, J., and McCartney, P. "Help!" [Recorded by The Beatles]. CD, *1*. United States: Capitol Records, 2000 (recorded 1965).

Lennon, J., McCartney, P., and Starr, R. "What Goes On." [Recorded by The Beatles]. CD, *Rubber Soul*. United States: Capitol Records, 1990 (recorded 1965).

Miller, T. K. (ed.). *The CAS Book of Professional Standards in Higher Education*. Washington, D.C.: Council for the Advancement of Standards in Higher Education, 2003.

Murphy, B. C., and Dillon, C. *Interviewing in Action: Relationship, Process, and Change.* (2nd ed.) Pacific Grove, Calif.: Brooks/Cole, 2003.

Ordinary People [motion picture]. United States: Paramount Pictures, 1980.

"Pilot" [television series episode]. *Felicity.* United States: Buena Vista Entertainment, 1998.

The Prince of Tides [motion picture]. United States: Columbia Pictures, 1991.

Solotaroff, P. *Group: Six People in Search of a Life.* New York: Riverhead Books, 1999.

"The Sopranos" [television series episode]. *The Sopranos.* United States: Home Box Office, 1999.

The Sopranos [television series]. United States: Home Box Office, 1999–2004.

Spice Girls, Stannard, R., and Rowe, M. "Wannabe." [Recorded by The Spice Girls]. Cassette, *Spice.* United States: Virgin Records America, 1996.

Strange, B., and Davis, S. "A Little Less Conversation." [Recorded by Elvis Presley]. CD, *Elvis—30 #1 Hits.* United States: RCA Records, 2002 (recorded 1968).

Styron, W. *Darkness Visible: A Memoir of Madness.* New York: Random House, 1990.

Three Approaches to Psychotherapy, Parts I, II, and III [videotape]. United States: Psychological & Educational Films, 1965.

Tin Cup [motion picture]. United States: Warner Brothers, 1996.

Tyler, J. M., and Reynolds, T. "Using Feature Films to Teach Group Counseling." *Journal for Specialists in Group Work,* 1998, 23(1), 7–21.

Wedding, D., and Boyd, M. A. *Movies and Mental Illness: Using Films to Understand Psychopathology.* Boston: McGraw-Hill College, 1999.

What About Bob? [motion picture]. United States: Touchstone Pictures, 1991.

Winston, R. B., Jr., and Fitch, R. T. "Paraprofessional Staffing." In R. B. Winston, Jr. and S. Anchors (eds.), *Student Housing and Residential Life: A Handbook for Professionals Committed to Student Development Goals.* San Francisco: Jossey-Bass, 1993.

Yager, G. G., Johns, B. D., Ingram, M. A., and Brown, R. "The Effect of Recognition of Counselor and Counselor Skill on Counselor Trainees' Ratings of a Videotaped Counselor Effectiveness." Paper presented at the annual meeting of the American Educational Research Association, San Francisco, 1995.

Yalom, I. D. *Lying on the Couch.* New York: Basic Books, 1996.

DEBORAH J. TAUB *is associate professor of educational studies at Purdue University in West Lafayette, Indiana.*

DEANNA S. FORNEY *is professor of college student personnel in the Department of Educational and Interdisciplinary Studies at Western Illinois University in Macomb, Illinois.*

8

Books, music, films and other media sources are identified in terms of their unique value in teaching career development.

Using Entertainment Media to Inform Student Affairs Teaching and Practice Related to Career Development

John C. Dagley, Pamela O. Paisley

"It is okay to think about what you want to do, until it is time to start doing what you were meant to do" (*The Rookie*, 2002). This scripted line of dialogue, delivered on two separate occasions in the movie *The Rookie,* provides the essence of the story line. Jimmy Morris, in his early thirties, struggles with whether he should follow his boyhood dream of becoming a baseball pitcher in the major leagues, which he gave up because of an injury to his pitching arm, long since healed, or be rational and continue to teach high school chemistry. The line, when delivered by the protagonist's father, seems to present the message that the son needs to quit thinking about what he *wants* to do, grow up, and get on with life. Interestingly, the opposite message is presented to millions of readers in the hugely popular annual edition of Bolles's job-hunting guide *What Color Is Your Parachute?* (Bolles, 2003).

Graduate students entering the student affairs profession often receive advice similar to that given by Jimmy Morris's father from their own parents, from peers, and from other well-intentioned individuals. These responses include "You are going into what?" "What is that?" "I know you enjoyed college, but you cannot stay in the ivory tower forever," and "You ought to go into the computer field."

Undergraduate students, as well, are often confronted with such comments. It was probably advice like that last statement about computers that made management information systems such a wildly popular major in the 1990s, only to bottom out near the end of the decade. It is interesting that so many people in our lives seem to feel as though they have ready solutions for our career dilemmas. It seems as though everyone is a vocational coach (Holland, 1973). Unfortunately, the coaching is not always sound or information-based. In fact, most coaching takes the form of advice, cheap advice, as it often turns out to be, in that more often than not it is a product of misinformation or simply no information. It is no wonder that students at all levels experience significant confusion and stress associated with educational and career choices.

The ultimate career development film, *The Graduate* (1967), is perhaps the most pure presentation of the overall angst and confusion the undecided college graduate faces in the struggle with thoughts about what to do with life after graduation. "Plastics," is the career advice offered the graduate in the film, much as today's graduate hears "computers," which is typically offered as a universal, one-size-fits-all suggestion without knowledge of supply and demand projections, competency requirements, degrees of personal interest, or any sense of the individual's primary life goals.

Evidence abounds that on today's campuses we can do a better job of meeting the career development needs of students. So how should we go about improving our services? What is known about career development that student affairs professionals need to know? What are the basic theoretical constructs and proven intervention strategies and techniques? With that knowledge as a base, how can we then use entertainment media to teach those constructs, strategies, and techniques?

Career Development Primer

Important concepts related to assisting students with the career development process are explained in this section.

Work as a Basic Need. Themes related to various aspects of work are omnipresent in the media of our time to a degree matched only by those dealing with human relationships. Perhaps work and relationships do indeed reflect two of the primary tasks of life, as hypothesized by Alfred Adler (1935). Certainly, today's college and university students fill student centers, coffeehouses, bars, and even some classes with conversations surrounding basic questions: "What am I going to do with the rest of my life? With whom am I going to live, and where?"

Students pursue higher education for a number of reasons, but the majority seem to matriculate for practical reasons ("Attitudes and Characteristics. . . . ," 2003). During the twentieth century, higher education institutions dramatically changed their focus, evolving from isolated *in loco parentis* campuses with classics-driven curricula to burgeoning centers of vocationalism where students of the twenty-first century expect to prepare for a career. Institutions of higher learning have become bastions of practicality, at least in the eyes of the students and their parents, if not in the eyes of the professors. Therein may lie the greatest challenge for today's student affairs professional. That is, while the students and parents have become increasingly committed to the practical side of collegiate study, colleges and universities have not uniformly reshaped their curricula or redistributed their resources accordingly. By default, student affairs professionals have become the frontline facilitators of students' career development.

Myths, Misconceptions, and Mistakes. Students come to campus with a number of myths and misconceptions that often compromise their decision-making ability. The first myth is that students should know which path is best for them. What do you want to major in? is a question that may seem simple at first glance, but it can feel like a sharp-edged sword to an undecided student. It is not as though one can simply look in a crystal ball and decide on the spot. In actuality, knowledge of educational and occupational preferences comes from leading a self-examined and self-reflective life. Over time, students learn to distinguish tasks and challenges that grab more of their spirit, elicit more of their best efforts, and provide more meaningful satisfaction.

Another myth is that one job by itself is sufficient to meet all of an individual's needs. That is a lot to ask of a job. Yet another myth is that one must not change majors because quitters never win. Students often finish out a major even though they may have declared the major several years earlier, at a time when they had less knowledge of their own interests, abilities, and opportunities. Abilities and interests are not always synonymous. While effort is of major importance, ability is oftentimes of more importance in pursuing educational and career options.

Other students make the mistake of pursuing career opportunities by default. Graduation time rolls around, and they still have no idea what they want to do, so they accept a position at the same place where they worked part-time during school. That way, they at least do not have to experience the rejection shock that tends to come with most job seeking. This low-risk approach to career choice reflects the seductive power of familiarity, reminiscent of the little boy who explained to his father after falling out of bed, "I guess I stayed too close to where I got in."

A final mistake worth mentioning is that too many students prepare for careers in fields chosen to meet the expectations or wishes of others. This has been an especially dramatic restriction for young women in our society, because they have been counseled toward secure and traditional employment in very limited fields. Vocational theorist Linda Gottfredson (1981, 2002) refers to this phenomenon as circumscription, wherein young women constrict their opportunities by overdeveloping thoughts about self formed by external sources and by underdeveloping personal cognitions that reflect a more efficacious private self. One of the central themes of the film *Legally Blonde* (2001) is the process (and importance) of breaking out of that set of restricted thoughts about self that has been imposed by both self and others.

Students carry other misconceptions of the career development process. In spite of the rapid pace of change in our society, students somehow conclude that their first decision about employment is going to be their last, as though career choice is a single, final decision at a prescribed point in time. This once-and-for-all thinking is a misconception that ratchets up the pressure of making the right choice, as though there is exactitude in choice, wherein one and only one job out there is just right. Unfortunately, some of today's collegians carry feelings of entitlement as well, expecting that employers will seek them out to offer the perfect job.

Once hired, students tend to enter their first job with unrealistic expectations about the work environment or what will be expected of them. Consequently, when some of the more mundane aspects of the daily work routine come into their lives or when their first negative encounters with supervisors occur, it is difficult for them to integrate these experiences with their previously cherished lofty ideals of work. The recent movie *Office Space* (1999) could be used to make this point with students. Almost every worker at some point in the beginning of his or her career feels like saying "I don't like my job, and I think I'm just going to stop going to work," as the main character in this film said after daily experiences on the lowest rung of the corporate ladder. Another line that is relevant to the interplay of life roles and career development comes near the end of the film, when the main character says to his girlfriend, "I may not ever be happy with my job, but I could be happy with life with you."

Theoretical Constructs. Convergences in career development theory and research (Savickas and Lent, 1994) enable us to present a brief set of theoretical constructs that have particular relevance for student affairs professionals. First, let us start with the term *career development.* Super (1957) was influential in helping the profession shift from seeing vocational choice as a once-in-a-lifetime decision to envisioning the process as developmental, consisting of identifiable stages with tasks to be accomplished within each stage. For example, he hypothesized and later empirically validated that students in late adolescence and early adulthood (the majority of college students) were in the exploration stage. As its name implied, exploration emphasized the role of investigating the relationship of studies to career options through internships, externships, and other practical applications of classroom studies. Super highlighted the importance of keeping options open and warned against prematurely foreclosing options through what he termed pseudocrystallization.

Student affairs professionals are all too familiar with painful examples of students who come to campus very comfortable with a definite choice of major and career, only to find that neither was anything like what they had imagined. For example, a large percentage of students who select pre-law, pre-med, pre-vet, or accounting courses do not complete their studies or actually practice, either because of a shift of interests or a mismatch with abilities. The career development process works most effectively when a person is able to experience work roles directly or vicariously, discuss their experiences with others, and then integrate those experiences within their own set of concepts about self. Super (1957) speculated that as individuals implement their self-concept in their career choice and as their self-concept matures, they confront a growing sense of multipotentiality in which the relationships of interests, abilities, and opportunities become increasingly complex.

As college students grow in their cognitive development (become more complex in their thinking), they are likely to shift from external career development resources (for example, parents or peers) to internal ones. In the process, they move from dualistic thinking dominated by such myths as exactitude and certainty, as outlined earlier in the chapter, to more multiplistic and relativistic thinking in which they feel more empowered to take charge of their own career development process.

Another construct of value in thinking about helping college students prepare for the work world is that one's career comprises more than just one's work role. Career can best be understood contextually as intertwined with and embedded within a multitude of roles, settings, and events (Gysbers and Moore, 1973; Hansen, 1997; Super, 1980, 1990). "While making a living, people live a life" (Savickas, 2002, p. 159).

Some students seem to learn from experience, and some do not. This reality may find origin in the maturity of perspective with which each makes self-observation generalizations (Krumboltz, 1979, 1994). Early in life, an individual begins to formulate thoughts about self that lead to an ever-growing internal vocabulary of self-talk. If the vocabulary includes empowering, enlightened constructs, the individual develops confidence in making changes and exploring new opportunities. If the vocabulary is filled with self-defeating terms, confidence is diminished. It is important to learn how to take advantage of opportunities that life presents to you. In order to identify chance opportunities, however, one needs to develop the prerequisite observational and task approach skills, such as analytical skills, cognitive and emotional reactions, and work habits and actions. To take advantage of serendipitous encounters, not only does one need to have developed the required skills, but one needs to feel efficacious in the use of such skills. Life is too complex to draw exact cause-and-effect relationships in career choice, but one is more likely to experience satisfaction and success if one learns how to learn. The way in which one approaches a learning task greatly influences the outcome of the task (Lent, Brown, and Hackett, 2002).

A final theoretical construct of particular value for student affairs professionals is that of understanding the relationship of personality development to vocational choice. Holland (1966, 1997) points out the importance of learning to discriminate between what you like and what you don't, what you're relatively good at and what you're not, and activities you prefer and those you don't. The degree to which you develop the ability to differentiate (make good career decisions because your personality type reflects your work environment) and the degree to which you are personally consistent (possess integration among your interests, values, skills, and preferences) govern the degree to which you will know how to pursue an occupation in a work environment that is most congruent with your personality type. The person-environment fit leads to greater satisfaction and success, all other variables being equal.

Career as Story. Every person has a life story, regardless of the number of chapters. One of the tasks of the student affairs professional is to help students develop a greater sense of their own story, including the chapters of the past, present, and projected future. Often, these stories can best be unfolded in response to stimuli provided by daily events or by best-sellers, television shows, or popular films. Unfortunately, storytellers do not always hear their own stories. It helps to have listeners who are schooled in theoretical constructs that provide convenient frameworks for hearing and understanding career stories.

Using Media to Facilitate an Understanding of Career Development

Career development refers to a complex interaction between persons (with particular experiences, values, and characteristics) and the multiple contexts in which they find themselves. Student affairs professionals actually support development in a variety of domains (for example, academic, personal, and social as well as career), but there may be no more important question that educators and helping professionals can assist young people in answering than "How will I lead my life?" In fact, it has been suggested that the pervasive nature of work in American culture results in career issues' affecting all other life roles (Super, 1957). In this particular domain, as student affairs professionals are preparing to determine their own career paths and to assist others in their development, several questions seem particularly significant. Why do people work? What meaning does work have in the life of an individual? How do choices related to work affect the quality of the lives people live? Struggling with the responses to these questions will provide student affairs professionals with the foundation to be self-reflective personally but also to advocate for others in relation to access, opportunity, and awareness. This foundation will also allow practitioners to design experiences and provide environments that encourage optimal career development.

These significant questions actually have very complicated answers. Consideration of the full breadth and depth of the implications can rarely be addressed in an introductory textbook. Fortunately, those texts can be supplemented with a variety of creative materials and media. Popular movies, videos, music, books, magazines, and television programs as well as a wide range of Internet sites provide excellent resources. This section will provide examples of both classic and current resources that can be used to help students and practitioners understand critical concepts and questions in career development.

Working: A Classic Resource. In 1972, Studs Terkel published a classic piece of oral history entitled *Working: People Talk About What They Do*

All Day and How They Feel About What They Do. The book chronicles interviews with over 120 individuals in a variety of work settings and life circumstances. Though published over thirty years ago, the collection of conversations provides a rich resource for considering the critical concepts and questions related to career development. This classic work has also generated other more current resources, such as a Broadway musical, a Web site (www.studsterkel.org), and a teaching guide (Ayers, 2001).

The book, *Working* (Terkel, 1972), is actually divided into nine books and includes interviews with individuals who were working in farming, communications, service delivery, the arts, the automobile industry, finance, publishing, maintenance, sports, and a variety of other fields. Individual interviewees range from stockbroker to prostitute to professor to janitor.

The stories highlight many of the significant issues and struggles related to work and career development. As a collection, the book represents a premier example of oral history. Terkel considered the basis of his findings less interviews than conversations:

> I realized quite early in this adventure that interviews, conventionally conducted, were meaningless. Conditioned clichés were certain to come. The question-and-answer technique may be of some value in determining favored detergents, toothpaste and deodorants, but not in the discovery of men and women. There were questions, of course. But they were casual in nature—at the beginning: the kind you would ask while having a drink with someone; the kind he would ask you. The talk was idiomatic rather than academic. In short, it was conversation. In time, the sluice gates of the damned up hurts and dreams were opened. [1972, pp. xx–xxi]

The quality of the methodology and the range and depth of the insights in this collection of conversations make it a wonderful foundation for both reading and research assignments for graduate students.

One way to use the resources related to *Working* would be to ask students to produce a set of video interviews. Student learning outcomes for this project would include (1) becoming familiar with a classic piece of journalism related to career issues, (2) becoming aware of a variety of work-related issues, (3) understanding the range and levels of meaning that work has in individuals' lives, (4) recognizing changes in society and the world of work during the last thirty years, (5) becoming familiar with the interview as a method of qualitative research, (6) developing confidence in their own interviewing abilities, (7) refining their abilities to work in large and small groups, and (8) increasing their knowledge and experience related to video production.

Class members could be introduced to this material by using the conceptual overview provided in the previous section as well as by using class time to visit Studs Terkel's Web site. The class would be divided into small groups to complete the video project, although several decisions would be made at the class level. The book would be required reading for the class and would be supplemented with the DVD and video. The class would review the table of contents during one of the first classes of the semester and make decisions concerning the books of focus. Each small group would be responsible for becoming the experts on one of the nine books. All students would be expected to read the introductory sections. As background, each student would also be expected to research Terkel's Web site and become knowledgeable about his biography and the context for the conversations.

Beyond focusing specifically on the text and related materials, each student would be expected to conduct a videotaped interview with a worker. Small groups of class members could develop initial questions and prompts, edit the examples, and present the product to the rest of the class at the end of the semester. An instructional technology consultant should be made available to support the development of the final project. Students would also be expected to participate in group discussions on such important questions as the following: Why do people work? What meaning does work have in the lives of the individuals you read about or interviewed? How do issues related to work affect the quality of life for the individuals you read about or interviewed?

Examples of Media Use in Workshops. Entertainment media can be used in a number of ways to help student affairs professionals conduct workshops in college and university residence halls to help students explore important aspects of the career development process such as decision making, major selection, looking for internships, résumé writing, and interviewing. Following are some examples that use a variety of media:

• Popular music is a great media source for facilitating student discussions. A simple but effective technique is to ask students to identify specific popular songs with career development relevance.

• Another instructional activity uses films. The facilitator provides small groups of students with a trivia contest wherein they are asked to identify films from script lines and then discuss the film's relevance to career development. For example, in what movie did the main character challenge his students with "Carpe diem, lads. Make your lives extraordinary" (*Dead Poets Society,* 1989), or similarly, in what movie did the main character in the midst of a bout of self-doubt say, "I'm tired of trying to be someone I'm not," to which a friend responds, "What if you're trying to be someone you are!"? (*Legally Blonde,* 2001).

Students can also be encouraged to see the connection of motion pictures with career roles and issues by asking them to identify motion pictures by themes instead of lines. For example, students could be asked to name a movie in which the main character demonstrated deep passion for his or her work, as in the motion picture featuring a second-generation owner of a small neighborhood bookstore (*You've Got Mail,* 1998); or a motion picture that showed a deep passion and commitment to teaching music (*Music of the Heart,* 1999); or a film that showed unplanned fulfillment through chance events in life (*Mr. Holland's Opus,* 1995).

The trivia quiz format can also be focused on the identification of films that represent strong career themes such as unemployment (*Tootsie,* 1982), role conflict (*Mrs. Doubtfire,* 1993), or the connection of personal courage with life and work (*The Legend of Bagger Vance,* 2000).

• In terms of work and life values, *Tuesdays with Morrie,* both the book (Albom, 1997) and the made-for-TV-movie (*Tuesdays with Morrie,* 1999) provide great opportunities to examine priorities and to raise questions about what students would like their lives to be about. The book or movie could be used as the impetus for discussions, self-reflection, interviews with a role model who has been significant in their life, or autobiographical and projective lifelines.

Summary

The complexities of the issues related to career development and choice can rarely be understood or embraced through the use of standard texts or experience alone. Instead, these texts must be supplemented with resources that make the issues and processes multidimensional. Popular media such as books, movies, magazines, music, and the Internet have the potential to engage graduate students in student affairs and the undergraduates with whom they will work in meaningful discussion and reflection.

References

Adler, A. "The Fundamental Views of Individual Psychology." *International Journal of Individual Psychology,* 1935, *1*(1), 5–8.

Albom, M. *Tuesdays with Morrie: An Old Man, a Young Man, and Life's Greatest Lesson.* New York: Doubleday, 1997.

"Attitudes and Characteristics of Freshmen at Four-Year Colleges, Fall 2002." *Chronicle of Higher Education,* Aug. 29, 2003, p. 17.

Ayers, R. *Working: A Teaching Guide.* New York: New Press, 2001.

Bolles, R. N. *The 2003 What Color Is Your Parachute?* Berkeley, Calif.: Ten Speed Press, 2003.

Dead Poets Society [motion picture]. United States: Touchstone Video, 1989.

Gottfredson, L. S. "Circumscription and Compromise: A Developmental Theory of Occupational Aspirations." *Journal of Counseling Psychology,* 1981, *28*(6), 545–579.

Gottfredson, L. S. "Gottfredson's Theory of Circumscription, Compromise, and Self-Creation." In D. Brown (ed.), *Career Choice and Development.* (4th ed.) San Francisco: Jossey-Bass, 2002.

The Graduate [motion picture]. United States: MGM/UA Studios, 1967.

Gysbers, N. C., and Moore, E. J. *Life Career Development: A Model.* Columbia: University of Missouri, 1973.

Hansen, L. S. *Integrative Life Planning: Critical Tasks for Career Development and Changing Life Patterns.* San Francisco: Jossey-Bass, 1997.

Holland, J. L. *The Psychology of Vocational Choice.* Waltham, Mass.: Blaisdell, 1966.

Holland, J. L. *Making Vocational Choices: A Theory of Careers.* Englewood Cliffs, N.J.: Prentice Hall, 1973.

Holland, J. L. *Making Vocational Choices: A Theory of Vocational Personalities and Work Environments.* (3rd ed.) Odessa, Fla.: Psychological Assessment Resources, 1997.

Krumboltz, J. D. "A Social Learning Theory of Career Decision-Making." In A. M. Mitchell, G. B. Jones, and J. D. Krumboltz (eds.), *Social Learning and Career Decision-Making*. Cranston, R.I.: Carroll Press, 1979.

Krumboltz, J. D. "Improving Career Development Theory from a Social Learning Perspective." In M. L. Savickas and R. W. Lent (eds.), *Convergence in Career Development Theories: Implications for Science and Practice*. Palo Alto, Calif.: Consulting Psychologists Press, 1994.

Legally Blonde [motion picture]. United States: MGM/UA Studios, 2001.

The Legend of Bagger Vance [motion picture]. United States: Dreamworks, 2000.

Lent, R. W., Brown, S. D., and Hackett, G. "Social Cognitive Career Theory." In D. Brown (ed.), *Career Choice and Development*. (4th ed.) San Francisco: Jossey-Bass, 2002.

Mr. Holland's Opus [motion picture]. United States: Hollywood Pictures, 1995.

Mrs. Doubtfire [motion picture]. United States: Twentieth Century Fox, 1993.

Music of the Heart [motion picture]. United States: Miramax, 1999.

Office Space [motion picture]. United States: Twentieth Century Fox, 1999.

The Rookie [motion picture]. United States: Walt Disney Pictures, 2002.

Savickas, M. L. "Career Construction: A Developmental Theory of Vocational Behavior." In D. Brown (ed.), *Career Choice and Development*. (4th ed.) San Francisco: Jossey-Bass, 2002.

Savickas, M. L., and Lent, R. W. (eds.). *Convergence in Career Development Theories: Implications for Science and Practice*. Palo Alto, Calif.: Consulting Psychologists Press, 1994.

Super, D. E. *The Psychology of Careers*. New York: HarperCollins, 1957.

Super, D. E. "A Life-Span, Life-Space Approach to Career Development." *Journal of Vocational Behavior*, 1980, 16(3), 282–298.

Super, D. E. "A Life-Span, Life-Space Approach to Career Development." In D. Brown and L. Brooks (eds.), *Career Choice and Development: Applying Contemporary Theories to Practice*. (2nd ed.) San Francisco: Jossey-Bass, 1990.

Terkel, S. *Working: People Talk About What They Do All Day and How They Feel About What They Do*. New York: Pantheon Books, 1972.

Tootsie [motion picture]. United States: Columbia Pictures, 1982.

Tuesdays with Morrie [television movie]. United States: Walt Disney Pictures, 1999.

You've Got Mail [motion picture]. United States: Warner Brothers, 1998.

JOHN C. DAGLEY *is associate professor of counseling and counseling psychology at Auburn University in Auburn, Alabama.*

PAMELA O. PAISLEY *is professor of counseling and human development services at the University of Georgia in Athens.*

9

This chapter offers tips and additional books, films, television shows, Web sites, and other media resources for teaching and training.

Conclusion and Additional Resources

Tony W. Cawthon, Deanna S. Forney, Ron Bramhall, John C. Dagley, Tracy L. Davis, Merrily S. Dunn, Kandace G. Hinton, Mary F. Howard-Hamilton, Timothy R. McMahon, Pamela O. Paisley, Deborah J. Taub

Using multimedia tools in teaching and training can be a powerful way of enhancing student learning. For graduate program faculty and student affairs practitioners, these tools can contribute greatly to training and teaching, especially in academic preparation, student leader training, and developmental programming.

Chapter authors provided specific examples of multimedia resources and how to use such tools in teaching and training environments. This concluding chapter addresses how to locate multimedia resources, offers final tips for multimedia use, and provides a supplemental listing of entertainment media that can be used.

Locating Resources

Being knowledgeable about resources to use is only part of the challenge when using multimedia in teaching and training. The more difficult challenge is often locating these items so that one can use them. One of the first questions to be answered is "Do you plan to use resources that can be rented or purchased, or do you plan to construct your own?"

Constructing Your Own Resources. With the advances in technology and the reduced costs associated with owning such technology, Tony Cawthon's experience is that individuals are increasingly electing to create their own teaching and training tools. The most common method is taping current television programs. Legally, taping television programs is an ambiguous area. The key issue associated with such taping is interpretation of copyright laws.

While understanding and interpreting copyright laws is beyond the scope of this sourcebook, when taping programs for educational use, the prudent student affairs professional should have a general understanding of the exception in the Copyright Act known as the "fair use" rule. Fair use allows limited use of copyrighted materials without permission for educational purposes.

To clarify this legal issue, educational organizations and copyright owners have created guidelines for recording of broadcast programming. These guidelines are not law and have not been tested in court, but they provide excellent information on using television shows from network stations (not pay stations), and they are generally accepted as representing minimal standards of fair use ("Copyright and Fair Use: Grading Teachers on Copyright Law—Videotaping for the Classroom," 2003). Basically, these guidelines state that nonprofit educational institutions can tape television programs from network television, but these tapes can only be maintained for forty-five days. If the show is being used for instructional purposes, it can be shown once during the first ten of the forty-five days. The guidelines do allow for a second showing of the tape if additional instruction is needed. After this initial ten-day period, the tape can only be used as part of the decision-making process about whether to permanently include it in the curriculum. If the taped television series is to be perpetually used in teaching and training, the show must be bought or the copyright secured ("Copyright and Fair Use: Educational Uses of NonCoursepack Materials," 2003).

While these guidelines are useful, they often raise more questions than they answer. To protect themselves legally, individuals are encouraged to become knowledgeable about basic copyright law and to contact their university attorney about specific questions and situations. As more television shows are released on DVD for purchasing, the need to tape television shows will decrease.

Renting or Purchasing Resources. Many individuals choose to rent or purchase resources for teaching and training. Summerfield (1993) identifies six sources for renting or purchasing resources: (1) public libraries, (2) college and university media centers, (3) reference books and directories of films and videos, (4) professional organizations, (5) distribution and production companies, and (6) local bookstores and video stores. Numerous Web sites also contain extensive information about resources.

In Tony Cawthon's experience, it is relatively easy to find information regarding films and books in bookstores and on the Internet; however, locating information on possible music resources is much harder. The following books and Web sites are recommended as aids in securing entertainment media tools. Videos or DVDs can be used in educational settings without restrictions as long as the item used is a legal copy, shown in a classroom or similar face-to-face instructional setting, identified as being used not for entertainment but for instructional purposes, and viewed in a location designed for instruction ("Copyright and Fair Use Guidelines for Teachers," n.d.).

Books

Bleiler, D. (ed.) *TLA Film, Video, and DVD Guide 2004.* New York: St. Martin's Press, 2003.
    Provides up-to-date information on video availability and pricing, as well as plot synopses of over 10,000 movies.

Bogdanov, V., Woodstra, C., and Erlewine, S. T. *All Music Guide.* (4th ed.) San Francisco, Calif.: Backbeat Books, 2001.
    Offers a comprehensive list of music from the database of the All Music Guide Web site. Presents over 20,000 recordings in sixteen major music genres. Also offers guidance in the following music genres: jazz, rock, blues, soul, country, hip hop, and electronica. Could be used to explore album and song background information.

Brooks, T., and Marsh, E. *The Complete Directory to Prime Time Network and Cable Shows, 1946–Present.* (8th ed.) New York: Random House, 2003.
    Includes all series telecast on prime-time commercial and cable television. Users can refer to this book for series synopses, cast listings, and broadcast dates.

Buckley, P. *The Rough Guide to Rock.* (3rd ed.) London: Rough Guides, 2003.
    Reviews the best of what is available for over 1,200 artists and bands. Provides readers with an overview of the album and insight into the music and its meaning.

Craddock, J. *VideoHound's Golden Movie Retriever 2005: The Complete Guide to Videocassette and DVD.* (14th ed.) Farmington Hills, Mich.: Gale Group, 2004.
    Offers information on over 26,000 movies. Indexes allow readers to search for information by category, awards, cast, director, writer, composer, and title. Also offers extensive information on companies and how to order movies and on Web sites related to movies.

Fox, K., and McDonaugh, M. (eds.) *TV Guide Film and Video Companion 2004.* New York: Barnes & Noble, 2003.
    Presents detailed information on 3,500 selected movies from 1930 to the present. Can be used to review film plots, casts, and music in the movie.

Frank, S. *Buyers Guide to Fifty Years of TV on Video*. Amherst, N.Y.: Prometheus Books, 1999.
Contains information on over 50,000 shows that have appeared on television from 1948 to the present. Provides information on how to secure hard-to-find television programs through mail order.

Gianakos, L. J. *Television Drama Series Programming: A Comprehensive Chronicle (1947–1986)*. 6 vols. Metuchen, N.J.: Scarecrow Press, 1980–1987.
Provides detailed information on all dramatic programming on network television stations and cable. Helpful to the novice who is seeking television shows to use in teaching and training.

Hesley, J. W., and Hesley, J. G. *Rent Two Films and Let's Talk in the Morning*. New York: Wiley, 1998.
Provides assistance on using films in the psychotherapeutic process. More than 100 film examples are provided, along with techniques on how to use them in therapy settings.

Irvin, J., and McLear, C. (eds.). *The Mojo Collection: The Ultimate Music Companion*. (3rd ed.) New York: Cannongate Books, 2003.
Lists over 700 pop albums that are considered masterpieces. Provides album title, artist, producer, and track listings. Particularly helpful in identifying tools for training and teaching are the narratives provided about the album and artist.

Katz, E., Klein, F., and Nolen, R. D. *The Film Encyclopedia*. (4th ed.) New York: HarperCollins, 2001.
Presents a comprehensive listing of over 7,000 entries related to the movie industry in encyclopedia (alphabetical) format. Contains heavily researched material and can serve as the essential movie guide for both the novice and the knowledgeable moviegoer.

Maltin, L. *Leonard Maltin's Movie and Video Guide 2004*. New York: Penguin Group, 2005.
Offers a listing of over 13,000 VHS and over 8,000 DVD movies. Provides extensive lists of mail-order sources of videos that can be rented or sold and of those in public domain. Complete contact information for these mail-order sources is also provided.

Martin, M., and Porter, M. *DVD and Video Guide 2005*. New York: Random House, 2004.
Whereas other movie guides list information on all films ever produced, this guide provides information only on movies that are available for video store rental or direct-mail purchase.

Nelmes, J. (ed.). *An Introduction to Film Studies*. (2nd ed.) New York: Routledge, 2001.
    Provides an introduction to the key components of film, including information on history of filmmaking, discussion of key concepts, and case studies and examples for using films in discussions.

Pym, J. *Time Out Film Guide*. New York: Penguin, 2003.
    Lists 15,000 films reviewed in the last fifteen years by Time Out critics. Contains an extensive list of international films. Reviews provide insight into movie plot and character development.

Scheuer, S. H., and Brill-Scheuer, A. *The Pocket Guide to Collecting Movies on DVD*. New York: Pocket Books, 2003.
    Designed to assist the novice movie collector in building a personal movie library.

Terrace, V. *Encyclopedia of Television Series: Series, Pilots, and Specials*, Vol. 1: *(1937–1973)*. New York: Zoetrope, 1985.

Terrace, V. *Encyclopedia of Television Series: Series, Pilots, and Specials*, Vol. 2: *(1974–1984)*. New York: Zoetrope, 1987.
    These two volumes chronicle and reference almost every show that has appeared on television. Users can refer to this book for extensive information about those television series.

Walker, J. (ed.). *Halliwell's Film Guide*. (19th ed.) New York: HarperCollins, 2003.
    Offers plot synopses, movie ratings, cast lists, running times, and an alphabetical listing of over 23,000 DVDs and videos.

Web Sites

Movie Collection Web site
    http://www.moviesunlimited.com
    Provides a comprehensive guide to all titles (film and television shows) currently on video. Helpful in locating hard-to-find titles. Movies that were never released on video or that have been discontinued are not included. Billed as largest video resource (70,000 videos).

Internet Movie Database
    http://www.imdb.com/
    Provides comprehensive information on films and entertainment individuals and companies. Includes a detailed list of videos for purchase, current movie and television news, and extensive information on independent films.

Netflix Inc.
http://www.netflix.com
Internet-only site. Customers pay a set fee and receive a certain number of DVDs to keep for viewing as long as they would like, without incurring late fees. Upon returning DVDs, the customer can request new ones to watch. Contains over 18,000 films that are rented without mailing charges.

Episode Guides
http://www.epguides.com
Contains episode lists for over 2,000 television shows. Provides detailed guides for over 500 shows. For the user who does not have a specific episode in mind to use for teaching and training, this site is helpful because it contains information such as episode titles, air dates, guest stars, and detailed plot summaries.

TV Tome
http://www.tvtome.com
Over 1,700 complete guides for current and past television shows and over 2,800 shows listed with partial information. Has a "show news" section that often contains information about availability of the show on DVD or VHS.

All Movie Guide
http://www.allmovie.com
Includes over 250,000 films in its database. Allows users to search films by genre. Useful information on new releases.

Critics Choice
http://www.ccvideo.com
Lists over 50,000 classic and newly released DVD and VHS movies. Offers an excellent selection of bargain-priced movies.

Facets Multimedia
http://www.facets.org/asticat
Provides details on independent and foreign films. Movies can be rented or purchased.

Video Vault
http://www.videovault.com/
Offers information on vintage films that are rare and unavailable. Includes details on foreign cinema.

Video Library
http://www.vlibrary.com/vlibrary/
Offers a free membership and specializes in renting, not purchasing, over 21,000 videos. Current fee is $6.00 per title. Useful in locating independent, art, and foreign films.

Barnes and Noble
   http://www.barnesandnoble.com

Amazon
   http://www.amazon.com
   Both sites include an extensive listing of books, films, and music that
can be purchased either new or used. Extremely easy to navigate.

Final Tips

For some individuals, consistently incorporating entertainment media tools
in their teaching and training is the norm; however, for others, using such
tools is a new undertaking. Whatever your experience, incorporating entertainment media tools in teaching and training is a powerful mechanism for
enhancing student learning. To achieve maximum results, we offer the following suggestions:

• Determine the type of entertainment media tool you wish to use in
teaching and training and your objectives for using it. It is apparent that a
number of popular resources can be adapted for instruction. By having clear
goals and objectives prior to selecting your tools, you will increase your
chances of incorporating appropriate tools and strengthening learning.

• Select entertainment media resources carefully; selecting appropriate resources is essential to success. Using the most convenient resources is
not always the best choice. It is important to obtain and use tools that
enhance the learning experience of participants and that maintain the audience's interest. The tools selected should be appropriate for the content area
of the learning experience and for the intended audience. Of course, Tony
Cawthon has found that students respond more positively to better-written
books and better-produced films.

• Prepare participants in advance for the use of entertainment media
tools. Often, the participants may be familiar with the resource being incorporated. It is imperative that they understand that while the tool has entertainment value, the purpose of using it in the classroom or workshop is to
enhance the educational experience.

• Be knowledgeable about the resources being incorporated into teaching and training. Before using a resource, familiarize yourself extensively
with it, to ensure that it has worth and value. Learn as much as you can
about the resource; this may require reading the book, listening to the
music, or viewing the movie multiple times prior to use with the participants. One strategy is to seek out others' reviews of the resource. Critics'
reviews of works provide insight and understanding.

• Remain flexible. While most individuals who use entertainment
media have specific procedures for incorporating them into teaching and
training, it is important to understand that we must be flexible about their
uses. What has worked in the past may not work this year. What worked

with one audience may not work with another. Allow participants to provide feedback on your choices, then determine how you can incorporate this feedback in subsequent uses.

Additional Resources

Numerous films, books, television shows, and musical recordings can be used to enhance student learning. In addition to the resources discussed in each chapter, the following entertainment media items are also recommended.

General Student or Young Adult Development

PSYCHOSOCIAL DEVELOPMENT
  Mona Lisa Smile (film)
  Dead Poets Society (film)
  The Lion King (film)
  The Breakfast Club (film)
  Dangerous Minds (film)
  Riding in Cars with Boys (film)
  Steel Magnolias (film)
  Save the Last Dance (film)
  Once and Again (television series)
  My So-Called Life (television series)
  Felicity (television series)
  The Paper Chase (film)
  Moo (book)

COGNITIVE DEVELOPMENT
  12 Angry Men (film)
  Schindler's List (film)
  Cheaters (film)
  Bend It Like Beckham (film)
  Waiting to Exhale (film)
  The Color Purple (film)
  Say Anything (film)
  Sixteen Candles (film)
  Under the Tuscan Sun (film)
  What's Love Got to Do with It (film)
  Training Day (film)
  Harry Potter and the Sorcerer's Stone (film, book)
  The Emperor's Club (film)

Multicultural

ASIAN AND ASIAN AMERICAN CULTURE
  Rabbit in the Moon (film)
  Better Luck Tomorrow (film)

Eat, Drink, Man, Woman (film)
Snow Falling on Cedars (film)

AMERICAN INDIAN
Primal Mind (film)
The Education of Little Tree (film, book)
Wiping the War Paint Off the Lens (book)

AFRICAN AMERICAN
A Family Thing (film)
The Long Walk Home (film)
White Man's Burden (film)
Dancing in September (film)
Rosewood (film)
Ethnic Notions (film)
School Daze (film)
A Hope in the Unseen (book)
Souls Looking Back (book)

LATINO AND LATINA
My Family, Mi Familia (film)
City of God (film)
Real Women Have Curves (film)
Luminarias (film)
My Viva Loca (film)
Stand and Deliver (film)
A Darker Shade of Crimson (book)

WHITE PRIVILEGE
Bowling for Columbine (film)
American History X (film)
Do The Right Thing (film)
"True Colors" (*ABC Prime Time* television episode)
"Equal But Separate" (*60 Minutes* television episode)

Lesbian, Gay, Bisexual, and Transgender
Big Eden (film)
Sum of Us (film)
Torch Song Trilogy (film)
Forbidden Love (film)
The Truth About Alex (film)
Kissing Jessica Stein (film)
The Business of Fancy Dancing (film)
Coming Out Under Fire (book)
Rubyfruit Jungle (book)

Queer as Folk (television program)
The Broken Hearts Club (film)

Gender

My Girl (film)
A Walk on the Moon (film)
Boys Don't Cry (film)
Nothing in Common (film)
City Slickers (film)
Waiting to Exhale (book)
Hannah and Her Sisters (film)
Thelma and Louise (film)

Leadership

COMMUNICATION SKILLS
Dances with Wolves (film)
Erin Brockovich (film)
Glengarry Glen Ross (film)
I Love Lucy (television series)
West Wing (television series)

CONFLICT RESOLUTION
Gorillas in the Mist (film)
Citizen Kane (film)
NYPD Blue (television series)
Star Trek (television series)

CREATIVITY, POWER, AND INFLUENCE
Mr. Mom (film)
Working Girl (film)

CRISIS MANAGEMENT
Norma Rae (film)
ER (television series)
The Perfect Storm (book, film)

DECISION MAKING
Aliens (film)
Wall Street (film)
Into Thin Air (book)

ETHICS
Dead Man Walking (film)
The Junction Boys (film)
Straight Man (book)

MOTIVATION
  Election (film)
  Finding Forrester (film)
  Buffy the Vampire Slayer (television series)
  Tuesdays with Morrie (book)

SELF-AWARENESS
  Field of Dreams (film)
  Babe (film)
  Alias (television series)
  Oh, the Places You'll Go (book)

TEAMS
  Bend It Like Beckham (film)
  The Breakfast Club (film)
  Designing Women (television series)
  Watership Down (book)

WOMEN IN LEADERSHIP
  A League of Their Own (film)
  Erin Brockovich (film)
  Sports Night (television series)

Career Development
LATE ADOLESCENCE AND WORK/EDUCATION TRANSITIONS
  American Graffiti (film)
  Rebel Without a Cause (film)
  The Breakfast Club (film)
  Sliding Doors (film)

SHIFTING ROLES OF WOMEN AND WORK
  Erin Brockovich (film)
  9 to 5 (film)
  Working Girl (film)
  Ruby in Paradise (film)

WORK AND FAMILY ISSUES
  The Doctor (film)
  The Turning Point (film)
  Multiplicity (film)

CAREER DEVELOPMENT AND MENTORING
  Finding Forrester (film)
  Good Will Hunting (film)

WORK AND ENVIRONMENTS
Wall Street (film)
Career Movies: American Business and the Success Mystique (book)

Counseling Skills
The Breakfast Club (film)
The Prince of Tides (film)
Ferris Bueller's Day Off (film)
Hoop Dreams (film)
Stand and Deliver (film)
Mask (film)
He Said, She Said (film)
Terms of Endearment (film)
Shadowlands (film)
The Big Chill (film)
Ordinary People (film)
Being There (film)
About Last Night (film)
Breaking Away (film)
Thelma and Louise (film)
"Do You Want to Know a Secret" (song)

References

"Copyright and Fair Use: Educational Uses of NonCoursepack Materials." [http://fairuse.stanford.edu/Copyright_and_Fair_Use_Overview/chapter7/7-b.html]. 2003. Retrieved March 2, 2004.

"Copyright and Fair Use: Grading Teachers on Copyright Law—Videotaping for the Classroom." [http://fairuse.stanford.edu/Copyright_and_Fair_Use_Overview/chapter0/0-e.html]. 2003. Retrieved March 2, 2004.

"Copyright and Fair Use Guidelines for Teachers." [http://www.mediafestival.org/copyrightchart.html]. n.d. Retrieved April 12, 2004.

Summerfield, E. *Crossing Cultures Through Film*. Yarmouth, Maine: Intercultural Press, 1993.

TONY W. CAWTHON *is associate professor of student affairs and unit coordinator in the Counselor Education Department at Clemson University in Clemson, South Carolina.*

DEANNA S. FORNEY *is professor of college student personnel in the Department of Educational and Interdisciplinary Studies at Western Illinois University in Macomb, Illinois.*

RON BRAMHALL *is a leadership and communication instructor in the Lundquist College of Business at the University of Oregon, Eugene.*

JOHN C. DAGLEY *is associate professor of counseling and counseling psychology at Auburn University in Auburn, Alabama.*

TRACY L. DAVIS *is associate professor of college student personnel in the Department of Educational and Interdisciplinary Studies at Western Illinois University in Macomb, Illinois.*

MERRILY S. DUNN *is assistant professor and program coordinator of the College Student Affairs Administration Program in the Department of Counseling and Human Development Services at the University of Georgia in Athens.*

KANDACE G. HINTON *is assistant professor in the Department of Educational Leadership, Administration, and Foundations, Higher Education and Administration Program at Indiana State University–Terre Haute.*

MARY F. HOWARD-HAMILTON *is associate dean of graduate studies in the School of Education and associate professor in the Department of Educational Leadership and Policy Studies, Higher Education and Student Affairs Program at Indiana University Bloomington.*

TIMOTHY R. MCMAHON *is a faculty consultant in the Teaching Effectiveness Program at the University of Oregon, Eugene.*

PAMELA O. PAISLEY *is professor of counseling and human development services at the University of Georgia in Athens.*

DEBORAH J. TAUB *is associate professor of educational studies at Purdue University in West Lafayette, Indiana.*

INDEX

Back Issue/Subscription Order Form

Copy or detach and send to:

Jossey-Bass, A Wiley Imprint, 989 Market Street, San Francisco CA, 94103-1741

Call or fax toll-free: Phone 888-378-2537 6:30AM – 3PM PST; Fax 888-481-2665

Back Issues: Please send me the following issues at $27 each
(Important: please include ISBN number with your order.)

_____

_____

_____

$ _____ Total for single issues

$ _____ SHIPPING CHARGES: SURFACE   Domestic Canadian
                                First Item $5.00 $6.00
                                Each Add'l Item $3.00 $1.50
For next-day and second-day delivery rates, call the number listed above.

Subscriptions   Please __ start __ renew my subscription to *New Directions for Student Services* for the year 2____at the following rate:

U.S.	__ Individual $75	__ Institutional $170
Canada	__ Individual $75	__ Institutional $210
All Others	__ Individual $99	__ Institutional $244
U.S. Online Subscription		__ Institutional $170
U.S. Print & Online Subscription		__ Institutional $187

**For more information about online subscriptions visit
www.wileyinterscience.com**

$ _____ Total single issues and subscriptions (Add appropriate sales tax for your state for single issue orders. No sales tax for U.S. subscriptions. Canadian residents, add GST for subscriptions and single issues.)

__Payment enclosed (U.S. check or money order only)
__VISA __ MC __ AmEx Card #_____Exp.Date_____

Signature _____Day Phone_____

__Bill Me (U.S. institutional orders only. Purchase order required.)

Purchase order # _____
                  Federal Tax ID13559302   **GST 89102 8052**

Name_____

Address_____

_____

Phone_____ E-mail _____

For more information about Jossey-Bass, visit our Web site at www.josseybass.com

SS107   Developing Effective Programs and Services for College Men
         Gar E. Kellom
         This volume's aim is to better understand the challenges facing college men,
         particularly at-risk men. Topics include enrollment, retention, academic
         performance, women's college perspectives, men's studies perspectives,
         men's health issues, emotional development, and spirituality. Delivers
         recommendations and examples about programs and services that improve
         college men's learning experiences and race, class, and gender awareness.
         ISBN: 0-7879-7772-1

SS106   Serving the Millennial Generation
         Michael D. Coomes, Robert DeBard
         Focuses on the next enrollment boom, students born after 1981, known as
         the Millennial generation. Examines these students' attitudes, beliefs, and
         behaviors, and makes recommendations to student affairs practitioners for
         working with them. Discusses historical and cultural influences that shape
         generations, demographics, teaching and learning patterns of Millennials,
         and how student affairs can best educate and serve them.
         ISBN: 0-7879-7606-7

SS105   Addressing the Unique Needs of Latino American Students
         Anna M. Ortiz
         Explores the experiences of the fast-growing population of Latinos in higher
         education, and what these students need from student affairs. This volume
         examines the influence of the Latino family, socioeconomic levels, cultural
         barriers, and other factors to understand the challenges faced by Latinos.
         Discusses administration, student groups, community colleges, support
         programs, cultural identity, Hispanic-Serving Institutions, and more.
         ISBN: 0-7879-7479-X

SS104   Meeting the Needs of African American Women
         Mary F. Howard-Hamilton
         Identifies and explores the critical needs for African American women as
         students, faculty, and administrators. This volume introduces theoretical
         frameworks and practical applications for addressing challenges; discusses
         identity and spirituality; explores the importance of programming support in
         recruitment and retention; describes the benefits of mentoring; and provides
         illuminating case studies of black women's issues in higher education.
         ISBN: 0-7879-7280-0

SS103   Contemporary Financial Issues in Student Affairs
         John H. Schuh
         This volume addresses the challenging financial situation facing higher
         education and offers creative solutions for student affairs staff. Topics
         include the differences between public and private institutions in funding
         student activities, how to demonstrate financial accountability to
         stakeholders, plus ways to address budget challenges in student unions,
         health centers, campus recreation, counseling centers, and student housing.
         ISBN: 0-7879-7173-1

SS102   **Meeting the Special Needs of Adult Students**
Deborah Kilgore, Penny J. Rice
This volume examines the ways student services professionals can best help
adult learners. Chapters highlight the specific challenges that adult
enrollment brings to traditional four-year and postgraduate institutions,
which are often focused on the traditional-aged student experience.
Explaining that adult students are typically involved in campus life in
different ways than younger students are, the volume provides student
services professionals with good guidance on serving an ever-growing
population.
ISBN: 0-7879-6991-5

SS101   **Planning and Achieving Successful Student Affairs Facilities Projects**
Jerry Price
Provides student affairs professionals with an examination of critical
facilities issues by exploring the experiences of their colleagues. Illustrates
that students' educational experiences are affected by residence halls,
student unions, dining services, recreation and wellness centers, and campus
grounds, and that student affairs professionals make valuable contributions
to the success of campus facility projects. Covers planning, budgeting,
collaboration, and communication through case studies and lessons learned.
ISBN: 0-7879-6847-1

SS100   **Student Affairs and External Relations**
Mary Beth Snyder
Building positive relations with external constituents is as important in
student affairs work as it is in any other university or college division. This
issue is a long-overdue resource of ideas, strategies, and information aimed
at making student affairs leaders more effective in their interactions with
important off-campus partners, supporters, and agencies. Chapter authors
explore the current challenges facing the student services profession as well
as the emerging opportunities worthy of student affairs interest.
ISBN: 0-7879-6342-9

SS99   **Addressing Contemporary Campus Safety Issues**
Christine K. Wilkinson, James A. Rund
Provided for practitioners as a resource book for both historical and evolving
issues, this guide covers hazing, parental partnerships, and collaborative
relationships between universities and the neighboring community.
Addressing a new definition of a safe campus environment, the editors have
identified topics such as the growth in study abroad, the implications of
increased usage of technology on campus, and campus response to
September 11. In addition, large-scale crisis responses to student riots and
multiple campus tragedies have been described in case studies. The issue
speaks to a more contemporary definition of a safe campus environment that
addresses not only physical safety issues but also those of a psychological
nature, a more diverse student body, and quality of life.
ISBN: 0-7879-6341-0

SS98   **The Art and Practical Wisdom of Student Affairs Leadership**
Jon Dalton, Marguerite McClinton
This issue collects reflections, stories, and advice about the art and practice
of student affairs leadership. Ten senior student affairs leaders were asked to
maintain a journal and record their personal reflections on practical wisdom

they have gained in the profession. The authors looked inside themselves to provide personal and candid insight into the convictions and values that have guided them in their work and lives.
ISBN: 0-7879-6340-2

SS97   **Working with Asian American College Students**
Marylu K. McEwen, Corinne Maekawa Kodama, Alvin N. Alvarez, Sunny Lee, Christopher T. H. Liang
Highlights the diversity of Asian American college students, analyzes the "model minority" myth and the stereotype of the "perfidious foreigner," and points out the need to consider the racial identity and racial consciousness of Asian American students. Various authors propose a model of Asian American student development, address issues of Asian Americans who are at educational risk, discuss the importance of integration and collaboration between student affairs and Asian American studies programs, and offer strategies for developing socially conscious Asian American student leaders.
ISBN: 0-7879-6292-9S

United States Postal Service

Statement of Ownership, Management, and Circulation

1. Publication Title	2. Publication Number	3. Filing Date
New Directions For Student Services	0 1 6 4 – 7 9 7 0	10/1/04

4. Issue Frequency	5. Number of Issues Published Annually	6. Annual Subscription Price
Quarterly	4	$170.00

7. Complete Mailing Address of Known Office of Publication (Not printer) (Street, city, county, state, and ZIP+4)

Wiley Subscription Services, Inc. at Jossey-Bass, 989 Market Street, San Francisco, CA 94103

Contact Person
Joe Schuman

Telephone
(415) 782-3232

8. Complete Mailing Address of Headquarters or General Business Office of Publisher (Not printer)

Wiley Subscription Services, Inc. 111 River Street, Hoboken, NJ 07030

9. Full Names and Complete Mailing Addresses of Publisher, Editor, and Managing Editor (Do not leave blank)

Publisher (Name and complete mailing address)

Wiley, San Francisco, 989 Market Street, San Francisco, CA 94103-1741

Editor (Name and complete mailing address)

John H. Schuh, N243 Lagomarcino Hall, Iowa State University, Ames, IA 50011

Managing Editor (Name and complete mailing address)

None

10. Owner (Do not leave blank. If the publication is owned by a corporation, give the name and address of the corporation immediately followed by the names and addresses of all stockholders owning or holding 1 percent or more of the total amount of stock. If not owned by a corporation, give the names and addresses of the individual owners. If owned by a partnership or other unincorporated firm, give its name and address as well as those of each individual owner. If the publication is published by a nonprofit organization, give its name and address.)

Full Name	Complete Mailing Address
Wiley Subscription Services, Inc.	111 River Street, Hoboken, NJ 07030
(see attached list)	

11. Known Bondholders, Mortgagees, and Other Security Holders Owning or Holding 1 Percent or More of Total Amount of Bonds, Mortgages, or Other Securities. If none, check box → ☑ None

Full Name	Complete Mailing Address
None	None

12. Tax Status (For completion by nonprofit organizations authorized to mail at nonprofit rates) (Check one)
The purpose, function, and nonprofit status of this organization and the exempt status for federal income tax purposes:
☐ Has Not Changed During Preceding 12 Months
☐ Has Changed During Preceding 12 Months (Publisher must submit explanation of change with this statement)

PS Form **3526**, October 1999 (See Instructions on Reverse)

---

3. Publication Title	14. Issue Date for Circulation Data Below
New Directions For Student Services	Summer 2004

5.	Extent and Nature of Circulation		Average No. Copies Each Issue During Preceding 12 Months	No. Copies of Single Issue Published Nearest to Filing Date
a.	Total Number of Copies (Net press run)		1641	1537
b. Paid and/or Requested Circulation	(1)	Paid/Requested Outside-County Mail Subscriptions Stated on Form 3541. (Include advertiser's proof and exchange copies)	600	580
	(2)	Paid In-County Subscriptions Stated on Form 3541 (Include advertiser's proof and exchange copies)	0	0
	(3)	Sales Through Dealers and Carriers, Street Vendors, Counter Sales, and Other Non-USPS Paid Distribution	0	0
	(4)	Other Classes Mailed Through the USPS	0	0
c.	Total Paid and/or Requested Circulation (Sum of 15b. (1), (2),(3),and (4)) ▲		600	580
d. Free Distribution by Mail (Samples, compliment ary, and other free)	(1)	Outside-County as Stated on Form 3541	0	0
	(2)	In-County as Stated on Form 3541	0	0
	(3)	Other Classes Mailed Through the USPS	0	0
e.	Free Distribution Outside the Mail (Carriers or other means)		101	110
f.	Total Free Distribution (Sum of 15d. and 15e.) ▲		101	110
g.	Total Distribution (Sum of 15c. and 15f) ▲		701	690
h.	Copies not Distributed		940	847
i.	Total (Sum of 15g. and h.) ▲		1641	1537
j.	Percent Paid and/or Requested Circulation (15c. divided by 15g. times 100)		86%	84%

16. Publication of Statement of Ownership
☑ Publication required. Will be printed in the Winter 2004 issue of this publication. ☐ Publication not required.

17. Signature and Title of Editor, Publisher, Business Manager, or Owner

Susan E. Lewis, VP & Publisher - Periodicals

Date 10/01/04

I certify that all information furnished on this form is true and complete. I understand that anyone who furnishes false or misleading information on this form or who omits material or information requested on the form may be subject to criminal sanctions (including fines and imprisonment) and/or civil sanctions (including civil penalties).

Instructions to Publishers

1. Complete and file one copy of this form with your postmaster annually on or before October 1. Keep a copy of the completed form for your records.

2. In cases where the stockholder or security holder is a trustee, include in items 10 and 11 the name of the person or corporation for whom the trustee is acting. Also include the names and addresses of individuals who are stockholders who own or hold 1 percent or more of the total amount of bonds, mortgages, or other securities of the publishing corporation. In item 11, if none, check the box. Use blank sheets if more space is required.

3. Be sure to furnish all circulation information called for in item 15. Free circulation must be shown in items 15d, e, and f.

4. Item 15h., Copies not Distributed, must include (1) newsstand copies originally stated on Form 3541, and returned to the publisher, (2) estimated returns from news agents, and (3), copies for office use, leftovers, spoiled, and all other copies not distributed.

5. If the publication had Periodicals authorization as a general or requester publication, this Statement of Ownership, Management, and Circulation must be published; it must be printed in any issue in October or, if the publication is not published during October, the first issue printed after October.

6. In item 16, indicate the date of the issue in which this Statement of Ownership will be published.

7. Item 17 must be signed.

Failure to file or publish a statement of ownership may lead to suspension of Periodicals authorization.

PS Form **3526**, October 1999 (Reverse)